Teenage Perspectives On The Black Experience In America:

An inside look at a groundbreaking high school course revealing the untold thoughts of students on the Black experience.

Jamaal C. Boyce

COPYRIGHT

Copyright © 2023 BY J Carmichael REI L.L.C.

All rights reserved. This publication, or any part thereof, may not be reproduced in any form, or by any means, including electronic, photographic, or mechanical, or by any sound recording system, or by any device for storage and retrieval of information, without the written permission of the copyright owner.

Printed in the United States of America

ISBN: 979-8-9870455-0-3 (Hard cover)

ISBN: 979-8-9870455-1-0 (Paperback)

ISBN: 979-8-9870455-2-7 (Ebook)

DEDICATION

This book is dedicated to Céline and DeVante Boyce. I hope this book inspires you to always THINK FOR YOURSELF. *Always question everything!!!!
Love you both.*

CONTENTS

PREFACE 5
01. WHY THE BLACK EXPERIENCE? 7
02. THE WORD BLACK 26
03. "BLACK" VS. "AFRICAN AMERICAN" 40
04. RACE: DOES IT EVEN EXIST? 51
05. RACISM: IS IT ACTUALLY HARMFUL? 68
06. THE "N-WORD" 99
07. STEREOTYPES OF BLACKS/AFRICAN AMERICANS 114
08. IMAGERY AND THE BLACK EXPERIENCE IN AMERICA .. 130
09. BLACK AMERICAN CULTURE: WHAT IS IT? 145
10. BLACK AMERICANS: VICTIMS OR VICTORS? 170
AFTERWORD 182

PREFACE

In a world full of opinions, one group's voices are constantly overlooked. This one group, it could be argued, is the most important as they will be the future of our society. Our young adults. What are they thinking? What is running through their minds? As a parent or an educator, how often do you discuss things with your children or students about what they may see in society? How is it affecting them? Are you challenging their train of thought? As educators and/or parents, are we giving them outlets to voice their thoughts and concerns? Do schools allow students the opportunity to discuss taboo topics that our children will have to face once they graduate high school?

This book was written as an extension of a high school course that I created titled **"The Black Experience in America For Secondary Education."** Critical Thinking and debate have always been a passion of mine. Over the course of my 20 years of teaching, I would always encourage my students to think critically and to challenge their way of thinking, and even to challenge me as the teacher. I noticed how much my students loved this style of teaching, and also how few if any classes allowed them to do so. That is why I created the class. To give a voice to the voiceless. This book was written to share their thoughts and hopefully inspire more adults to pay attention to the mindset of our youth and to challenge their way of thinking to get them to be better adults.

Each chapter in the book is based on a topic that was analyzed, debated, and discussed by my students and myself. As it is a critical thinking course, students were encouraged to freely voice their thoughts and beliefs on "controversial" topics that are rarely discussed in the classroom or at home. My students—of all different races—spoke from their own thoughts and experiences. Their answers are bound to surprise—and to make readers think and re-think, their own preconceived notions. This book tells the story of how I came to create the class, with extended excerpts from the many subjects that were discussed, and of the reaction to the course from students, myself, and the larger public.

My name is Jamaal C. Boyce, a high school teacher in Long Island, NY. My experiences as a Black man, and as one of the few Black male high school teachers in America, makes me uniquely qualified to examine these subjects with my students, as well as my over 20 years of experience in the field of public education. With many states looking to make ethnic studies a requirement for high school graduation, this book is aimed at an audience of educators, parents, students, or ANYONE who loves to think critically. -Jamaal C. Boyce

CHAPTER ONE
WHY THE BLACK EXPERIENCE?

I am a 41-year-old "Black/African American" man living on Long Island. I have been teaching for approximately 19 years in a district that is considered diverse and/or multicultural, depending on the term you choose to use. I've taught Global History 9, Global History 10, Participation in Government, Economics, ELL classes, alternative education, and a new course that I created for the 2021-2022 school year called "The Black Experience in America for Secondary Education," or simply "The Black Experience In America." More on that in a bit.

Over the course of these 19 years, I have learned a lot about public education. I have come into contact with many different types of people. When you teach in a public high school, just when you think you've seen it all, something new happens that you just can't believe. Education classes in college can NEVER truly prepare you for teaching. Actual teaching will prepare you for teaching. Teaching in a public school has many challenges. There are many successes that come through public education. There are also many failures, and that is where this book comes into play. In my time teaching, there are many observations I have made about public education in the United States. These observations are pretty much the same observations that I have about the United States in general.

There are very few Black/African American educators in the United States. According to a Pew Research Center article in 2021, only 7% of public school teachers are Black. There are apparently even fewer Black/African American male educators. In the United States, according to nynmedia.com, of those 7% of Black public high school teachers, only 2% are Black men. According to pewresearch.org, 79% of all public school teachers are White, while only 47% of the students in public schools in America are White as well. This would mean that the majority of students in American public schools are NOT White.

Also, according to zippa.com/teacher-jobs/demographics, 74.3% of all teachers are women as of the year 2021. My profession is dominated by White females. What effect can these teacher demographics have on students in our public schools? Not just the Black students, but ALL students? This is NOT a criticism. Just an observation. Is it a good thing? Is it a bad thing? I am not here to answer that. Should it matter? Do I have an opinion? Yes, I do. Will you know my opinion from reading this book? No. The fact of the matter is, I am one of the few of my kind in my profession. It is what it is. I am paid to do a job, and I do the job that I am paid to do to the best of my ability.

A WORD ABOUT INDOCTRINATION

I have made many observations within public education. I could list many, but my observations on public education are not the focus of this book. There is one thing I believe to be common across most high schools in America. Public education seems to be heavy on indoctrination. It is one of the main issues I have with the United States as a whole. What is the definition of indoctrination? Here are some definitions that I have found doing a basic Google search:

-the act of indoctrinating or teaching or inculcating a doctrine, principle, or ideology, especially one with a specific point of view (Dictionary.com)

-the process of repeating an idea or belief to someone until they accept it without criticism (Dictionary.cambridge.org)

-teaching someone to accept a set of beliefs without questioning them (Vocabulary.com)

Schools are very good at indoctrination. Schools can be boxes that cut off and protect their students. In fact, many high schools operate in contrast to the outside world. By design. Many schools graduate students who in most cases are sheep into a world full of wolves. Students are allowed to think to a certain extent, but they have very little opportunity in most cases to THINK CRITICALLY. Every morning at the beginning of the day, students stand for the Pledge of Allegiance. Without thinking, as if they had been programmed, they recite the same words day after day. If you were to watch from outside and had no idea it was about a pledge, you might think it was something out of a cult. Why? I guess to show their "loyalty" to our nation. OK, I get it. I've asked my students why they stand and say the pledge every morning. Almost none of them has had a real answer. In fact, a common answer was "my teachers told me to."

I am not suggesting students do not stand and say the Pledge of Allegiance. Couldn't this be a type of indoctrination? Couldn't a person argue that from the very start of the school day, students are being indoctrinated? Do five-year-olds in a kindergarten class understand what they are saying when they recite the Pledge of Allegiance? Is a student who sits for the pledge any less "loyal" or "patriotic" than a student who stands? For all we know, the student sitting for the pledge may plan to join the Marines and possibly be sent off to fight for our nation while the student who repeatedly stands and says the pledge may have no intention of doing anything of that nature. Neither of them is wrong, but with indoctrination, you are taught to think that if you do not conform to a societal norm something is wrong with you. Thinking outside the box is bad.

It's amazing we will stand every day without thought and pledge allegiance to our nation (again I'm not saying this is wrong), but we'll leave the house and not tell our family members we love them. As a parent, it is possible that over the course of a school year, your child will say the Pledge of Allegiance more than they will tell you that they love you. Have you ever thought about that? Is it even necessary to say the Pledge of Allegiance every day before classes start? Why? Does it make our students more patriotic? Is it possible that a student standing for the Pledge of Allegiance could despise America? Does standing for it absolve him or her of their hatred for the nation? How do you measure how "patriotic" someone is? While we are at it, why not play the national anthem every day before school? Would that be too much? If you believe THAT is too much, couldn't I then say that YOU are unpatriotic? Who determines these things?

One time, my students stood for the pledge, some barely even uttering it, others not even looking at the flag, and some on their cell phones as they did it. I had a discussion with my students and asked them, "If America were attacked and invaded, how many of you would volunteer and fight risking your life to defend the country?" Only two of the 33 students raised their hands. However, all 33 students 10 minutes earlier pledged allegiance to the United States of America. How many people pledge allegiance to America or stand for the national anthem but cheat on their taxes? How many so-called Christians will say the Pledge of Allegiance without thought, yet they didn't pledge allegiance to their own god that morning, let alone pray? Whether people should say the Pledge of Allegiance or not is a personal choice. I am NOT condemning the Pledge of Allegiance, but one cannot ignore the fact that each school day does start with some level of indoctrination.

Students are taught that the Hitler Youth in 1930s and 1940s Germany were indoctrinated to pledge allegiance to the fascist dictator (Adolf Hitler). Some people will argue that Hitler Youth were taught to hate. Weren't students in schools in the 1960s, '70s and '80s taught to fear and hate the Soviet Union? How are our students today being taught in school differently than students in say, China? I'm not saying they aren't. I'm asking how is it different. Explain it in detail. Then question your own explanation. Remember I never said it isn't different. I'm posing a question.

Youth in the United States are taught (or indoctrinated) to pledge allegiance to the nation. (It's different of course if you ask most Americans. I'm sure it is. Just explain how.) A teacher teaches a subject in most cases and administers a test. Formal tests of right and wrong questions and answers are constantly given. Where is the room for outside thinking or criticism of what is being taught? Not to say that schools should stop doing this. Do schools need tests? Absolutely. Tests can check to see if a student has gained the knowledge necessary to move on to a higher grade or position. I pray that the doctor who is performing surgery on me has passed his or her medical exams. However, shouldn't doctors be allowed to question different types of medicine that may be beneficial for patients, and discuss and debate them? Is there no room for this? Scientists must pass certain tests, of course. Shouldn't they also be allowed to discuss and debate certain topics in science, instead of having one universal idea? Most primary and especially secondary education in America does not have this balance. Most education at the high school level is geared towards testing and conforming to one idea. It is unbalanced. The issue is there really isn't much opportunity for critical thinking.

Now to my subject, history. I have never witnessed most of the events that I teach. How do I know that these events happened outside of learning it from someone else? Yes, there is plenty of historical evidence. However, what actual proof can I provide to a group of students in my classroom? The ability to critique really isn't an option.

Sure we can discuss things, but in the end, I must get back to the curriculum to make sure they pass their Regents(NY State test).

When I taught Global History 10, one of the first topics I would have to teach was the Scientific Revolution. It would be at the beginning of the year before the students got to know me. I would tell them for example, that I was a former CIA spy who went around the world and served in Iraq, or I was in the Air Force and flew B52 bombers with nuclear weapons. Neither was even close to being true. They believed it and would even ask me questions to elaborate. The next day I would expose my lies. The students couldn't believe that I as a teacher would lie to them, but I was proving a point. I told the class complete nonsense. They were so indoctrinated, they didn't even think to question my credentials. They just took what I told them and accepted it.

I would also ask my students if the Earth is round or flat. Of course, they would say it is round. I would then ask them to prove it right there and then and I would hand $20 to whoever could do so. They would try to prove it. It never worked. They would say you could see from a spaceship. Clearly, there wasn't a spaceship in the class so that was not proof. They would say look at the globe. My response was, "OK, the globe is round, what does that have to do with Earth?" They would say when you go on a ship, and I would stop them and say we don't have a ship in class so it's not proof. They would say look at a satellite image or a picture and I would say it was doctored not proof. Then they would say, prove the earth is flat, and I would simply ask them if the ground they walked in on was round or flat. They said flat, clearly, and I would say well, there is your proof.

In 17 years of teaching Global History 10 and that lesson, not one student could prove it in the class. Almost none of them ever looked through a telescope. For most of them, they were just regurgitating something they were told at a young age: that Earth was round, and they never questioned or challenged it. Now I am not a Flat Earther. I'm just proving a point. Students and people are designed to think to a certain degree, but they are NOT taught to think critically. America isn't a nation of people; it is a nation of puppets. Most people are just regurgitating what they've heard someone else say. My observations with schools, which permeate through our nation, is WE DON'T TEACH STUDENTS TO THINK CRITICALLY.

So, how is critical thinking defined? Using a google search, here are two simple definitions.

Critical Thinking

-disciplined thinking that is clear, rational, open-minded, and informed by evidence (Dictionary.com)

-the process of thinking carefully about a subject or idea, without allowing feelings or opinions to affect you (Dictionary.cambridge.org)

There are several other definitions of critical thinking. One thing that is certain is that all people are born with the ability to think. It is instinctive. However, critical thinking must be taught. Where are we supposed to learn this ability to critically think? Some will say in the home, but if the parents had the same schooling as their children, when would they have had an opportunity to learn how to think critically? Critical thinkers question everything they see and hear. As the old saying goes, a question opens the mind, a statement closes it.

Critical thinkers are constantly questioning commonly held beliefs. They even question their own beliefs. Think back. When did you learn more in your life? From birth to the age of five, or from the ages of 12 to 17? Virtually everything you learned to do, from walking and talking to coloring, you can still do today. If I gave adults a history or a chemistry test they took in high school, most would fail. Did you really learn anything? What's the common denominator? School. From birth to the age of five most kids are not in a formal school structure. From the ages of 12 to 17, they are. Also, from the time they can talk, what are young children constantly doing? Asking questions.

Even in a child's early years of schooling when they are in pre-K and kindergarten through elementary school, students learn and retain tons of information. It seems however, that the longer they are in school, the more indoctrination sinks in. It is easier for a young child to learn multiple languages than a middle-aged person. At my age, for me to learn Mandarin or Russian, I would have to battle the English that is deep-rooted in my old brain. A one-year-old whose brain is free and clear could probably learn both very effectively if it is simply spoken around them constantly. Young children constantly open their minds with questions. Teenagers, however, tend not to ask questions at least to the degree they did when they were younger. Are schools challenging students to think critically and ask questions? Schools most certainly are teaching, but are students learning? What are they learning? When students graduate, there is a commencement ceremony to celebrate the graduation. If you look up the word commence, it means to begin something. Why would a commencement ceremony be held after you have completed school, if commence means to begin? When you graduate from school, THAT is the beginning of learning, not when you start school. You will learn more OUTSIDE of school than in it. Critical thinking is essential to life long learning.

The more I taught, the more I noticed most of my students lacked the ability to think critically. They would make statements, and I would ask them a simple question challenging their statements and they had no answer. They would just say "because it is." They had no proof or evidence to fall back on. As stated earlier, many people in this country are puppets. They have puppeteers in their lives who have control over what they are saying. People are just regurgitating the words of someone else. When the puppeteer is absent, and you ask the puppets to elaborate on what they are saying, or you challenge it, these people either shut down or get angry because they don't know how to respond. They don't know how to think critically.

A person who thinks critically can debate anything they have knowledge about. They don't get angry when challenged because a person who thinks critically already knows the flaws in their argument. They already know how you will critique what they are saying and have a retort for your critique. They understand that what they are saying or believe has many different angles and what they believe almost certainly is flawed, as is everything else. Critical thinkers acknowledge that even though they have a belief about something, they could be wrong. They are playing chess while others can't even play checkers. In a debate, neither side is wrong if there is evidence to support their angle on how they see a certain topic. The fact that critical thinkers know the flaws in their argument and can acknowledge it means that they must have a certain level of humility. Most people you talk to do not have this humbleness. They are not critical thinkers. Thinkers maybe, but not critical thinkers.

Critical thinkers understand that there are MANY different perspectives on things. Many different angles. There is no such thing as a good or bad number. Numbers are just numbers. To get my students to understand different perspectives, I would ask them if 5 is equal to 10. They would say no. I would then ask them which is the better number. They would all respond, number 10, obviously, because it is bigger. I would then say, Great, and ask, would you rather be $10 million in debt or $5 million in debt? They responded with $5 million in debt. I would then ask, why did you tell me 10 was the better number? They would have an Aha! moment. It opened their eyes to the idea that there are different perspectives on everything.

In many cases, the issue is neither good nor bad. It just depends on your perspective, and looking at the issue from a different perspective is critical. I would also ask them to describe a dangerous animal. They would always name a large animal such as a shark, a tiger, or a lion. I would ask them, "How about a mosquito?" My students would look at me like I was crazy. Mosquitoes are tiny. How are they dangerous? Using a quick Google search, I showed them that mosquitoes generally kill more people than any other animal in the world. They never looked at the perspective that it can be the smallest creatures that are the most dangerous.

As time went on in my teaching career, I tried to get my students to think critically as much as I could. The problem was that the classes I taught only allowed for a certain level of critical thinking. As I have gotten older and moved away from traditional education, I've found myself reading contrasting viewpoints on many different topics. I've watched videos and debates on a variety of different issues. I began to understand that there is more than one side to a story. I began to question more and more things. I also began to think freely. I believed that I did not learn how to think critically until I left school. Searching for answers on my own helped me to learn to think for myself and challenge my previous beliefs and thoughts. In my Global History classes, I had a hard-structured curriculum that needed to be followed. Students needed to pass the state test at the end of the year. How much critical thinking could I require of them? If all I taught them to do was think critically but they didn't know what Realpolitik was, they might fail the state exam. They fail, and it hurts their chances of graduation. I was limited to only a certain level of critical thinking in my classes. I was looking to challenge my students more, and I was getting upset that I couldn't. Then something happened at the beginning of the 2020-2021 school year that I could never have foreseen.

A NEW COURSE: "THE BLACK EXPERIENCE IN AMERICA FOR SECONDARY EDUCATION"

The 2020-2021 school year was my 18th year in education. It started similarly to all other school years in my district. One day early in the year I was asked to stop by my principal's office. He asked me if I would be interested in being a part of celebrations that year related to the Black/African American population in my district. He said that a student I had the previous year had recommended me and said I would be a great influence. I was flattered. I said, "Sure, whatever you need me to do if I am able, I will do it." I left and went about my business.

Not long after, I got an email from members of the Black community asking me about teaching a course that we had in our high school called "African American History and Literature." The course had been around for a few years. It didn't have many students in it. At first, I thought it was a spam email and I deleted it. A few weeks later I got another email, and I went back to my principal and asked him about it. He informed me that members of the Black community specifically wanted me to teach the course. Why me? He explained that the community wanted an African American to teach the course. My initial reaction was to say no. I had no interest. Many people will read that and ask, "How could a Black educator have no interest in teaching an African American history course?" There are several reasons.

First, my schedule was set. I finally had all the classes that I wanted, and I was happy. Second, most of the students in the high school really had no interest in taking the course. Many people are shocked by that. I've heard many people say they can't believe that Black students aren't more excited to learn about Black history. My response to that is, "are White students eager to learn about White history?" Why would a Black student in today's age of social media, TV, cell phones, and other things that distract their minds be any more excited to learn about James Weldon Johnson than a White student is to learn about Lyndon Baines Johnson? Should they care? Teenagers are teenagers. Teenage students in general are not too excited about learning history, whether it is theirs or someone else's. When I taught Latin American Revolutions in Global History 10, my Hispanic students were no more or less interested than my Black/African American students were in learning about imperialism in Africa. The third reason I had no interest in teaching the "African American History and Literature" course was that it was another history class. Again, many students do not like history in general. They don't see the point. In fact, most people don't appreciate history until they are older. I wasn't interested in doing something "different" that was the same.

The fourth and probably the most important reason I had no interest is that I didn't want to be used as a pawn. I didn't want to be the "Black teacher" teaching the "African American History and Literature" course just so that it could be said that our school had an "African American History and Literature" course to show and placate certain members in the public. That would be insulting. I wanted to make an impactful positive change, not a change that yielded the same results. Another history class, this time with a Black person teaching it, but in the end only a few students taking it who were all Black. Not interested. My answer was no.

As time went on, pressure started mounting in the district and I was asked again if I would reconsider. I had a lot of internal conflict about this. So I came up with a no-lose situation for myself. I would try to make an impactful change. What I would come up with would be so different, radical, and new that they would either let me do what I proposed or say absolutely not and I never would have to worry about being asked to teach this class again. I met with another administrator and explained my reservations. I explained to her that I had a totally different idea. I told her that instead of teaching "African American History and Literature" (I'm not an English teacher, so the literature aspect is not really my forte), I wanted to teach a course called "The Black Experience In America!"

I changed the title of the course for a couple of reasons. Everyone has heard of a course called "African American History." It doesn't catch the attention of most people however, the word BLACK is different. You can't help but notice Black. The title "The Black Experience in America" makes you pause. What could that be about? No mention of history (even though history would be an element in the course) or literature. It's linked neither to history nor English. It stands out in a crowd. I also wanted to examine the many different experiences of so-called Black/African American people. History is a part of it, but it is not a history course. The administrator was very open to it and loved the idea. I listed the topics that I wanted to discuss in the course. This is where things got interesting. This is where I thought I would be told no because it would be considered too controversial. I thought this is where the issue would die, and I could go about the business of doing my job and being left alone. Some of the things I listed to discuss with my students were:

Black Lives Matter

Critical Race Theory

Black History Month: Is It Necessary?

Discussions on Slavery

Differences among Black/African Americans

Reparations For Black/African Americans

Race

Racism

Stereotypes of Black people

The N-Word

Dating/Relationships in the Black Community

Civil Rights Ideology (Malcolm X v MLK Jr.)

Is America a Racist Nation?

Police and the Black Experience

Segregation vs. Integration: Which is better for Black Americans?

There would be other things discussed in the course. Among them were Black Americans and Investing, Mental Health, Violence in Black Communities, The Black Family, and The Black Church. The items on the list were the items I thought would stand out and most likely be considered "controversial." I explained to her that I would not be indoctrinating the students. The course and its topics would be used as a tool to get students to learn how to think critically and understand there are many different angles and aspects to each topic, including among Black/African Americans. I was somewhat surprised that the administrator still loved the idea after she heard the topics.

This meeting took place in March 2021. She told me to send her the information about the proposed new course, "The Black Experience in America" in an email, and she would forward it to me as well as her superiors for the 2021-2022 school year. She sent the proposal to her superiors. We waited and waited and heard nothing back. We both threw our hands up and said, "It is what it is." In my mind, I had a smile. My plan worked. I was either going to do something different or they would leave me alone. Now they would say no way to my proposal and finally leave me alone. Either way, I won.

Fast forward to the end of April of the 2020-2021 school year. Another teacher says to me in passing, "Hey, congratulations, I hear you are teaching a new course." My reaction was shock. I didn't know what he was talking about. I went to my administrator and asked her about it. She said "The Black Experience in America" course had been approved for the 2021-2022 school year. I was completely caught off guard. I asked her if the district read my proposal and what I would be discussing in the class. She told me they had, and they loved it. I had full control over the course and I had their backing. Again, I was shocked. Now I had to teach the course. However, I was very nervous.

I prided myself on people not knowing who I was in the district. For 18 years I was able to stay off the radar. Most members of the community, in the district office or on the board of education in my district, hadn't a clue as to who I was. Now, with a course like this and sensitive subject matter, people would know. I confided in the people closest to me about my fears. I thought people would call for my job. I thought people at board meetings would destroy my name. I hate being known. Those close to me told me I had to do it because I could make a change. They said it was my duty as an educator to make a change when I had the chance. This was my chance to bring more critical thinking into the classroom. What I had been complaining about for several years I finally had a chance to do something about. I couldn't say no now. There was no turning back. My stomach was in knots.

My district allowed me to create the curriculum of my choice. I had complete creative control. Student scheduling for the following school year was winding down and a couple of my former students heard that I was teaching "African American History" and decided to sign up. I had to get the word out that the course was going in a different direction. I created rules for the course before it even began. It was an elective already, so I allowed only juniors and seniors to take the class. I also wanted to talk to the parents of every student before they signed up to let them know the changes that were occurring. I felt parents and students had to know that the course was going in a different direction, and I believed it would add a level of protection for me. If parents knew some of the subject matter beforehand, then they could not get angry at any discussions in the class. By the time I created these rules and conveyed them to my superiors, it was too late. A few students were already assigned to the class. It was still being called "African American History and Literature" because it was too late to change the name of the course in the school's course booklet. Things were not starting off well. I was not too excited.

The district was still supporting me in anything I needed. That summer, I started writing a curriculum for the course. I picked topics and issues about the experiences of Black/African Americans I believed would be a good tool to get my students to think critically. Over the course of the summer, I contacted the parents of the students in the class and explained the changes to them. They were all supportive. I was still nervous. Nobody in the community knew about the change.

With what I was discussing, I believed that members of the community would believe I was indoctrinating my students instead of getting them to think critically. I contacted my union and secured their support for what I feared would be an onslaught of bad publicity.

At the time the course was being created, Critical Race Theory was a hotly debated topic around the country. Parents would show up to board meetings railing against it. I know that people in America get VERY uncomfortable about conversations around race. I believed that when parents heard that a Black teacher was discussing race and racism, they would make assumptions. I knew that members of the community would have an issue with it. I prepared myself for it. I made sure to have the backing of my superiors, my union, and influential members of the community. I knew it was coming. I was ready and set for some ignorant person to say I am teaching Critical Race Theory even though many of the people I have heard criticize it have never been able to provide the actual curriculum as I don't know what is taught within its curriculum. It didn't matter. I knew people in the community with no evidence would say that is what I was doing.

I wrote a curriculum that was not finished but would be ready for the start of the school year. Originally, I had five students. By the end of the first year, three more would join for a total of eight. I had five Black students, two Hispanic students, and one Native American student. Six girls and two boys. I liked having a small class. It was an intimate setting that would allow students to speak freely. I truly believe most students are not ready for a course like this. Maybe 20% of high school students are mature enough for what I was trying to do. Truth be told, I would argue fewer than 10% of adults could handle what I was doing in the course. Why? Again, INDOCTRINATION. The more years of indoctrination a person has, the harder it is to get them to think from a different perspective. A 34-year-old adult has had 17 extra years of indoctrination as opposed to a 17-year-old. A 17-year-old has had 10 more years of indoctrination than a 7-year-old. Imagine the mindset of the average 50-year-old. The younger the mind, the more open-minded the mind is in general. Mind programming and indoctrination haven't had time to sink in with the lack of time. As people get older, they ask fewer questions and make more statements.

Critical thinking is all about asking questions. Questions force you to think and find answers. Critical thinkers do not get emotional in debates or discussions. I wanted to limit the number of students in the class. I wanted no more than 12 students at most. I didn't want this course to become a dumping ground for 33 students who wouldn't take it seriously. That's what many other classes are like. Eight students seemed perfect. Most people in this country are not ready for what I am trying to do.

Late that August I had everything ready to go for the new course, "THE BLACK EXPERIENCE IN AMERICA FOR SECONDARY EDUCATION." Here is the course description:

This course will examine the different experiences, perspectives, and cultures of so-called Black/African Americans from the early beginnings of America to the present day. The course will examine many different aspects of Black people and Black culture and will also examine the struggles as well as the triumphs of Black/African Americans through many different lenses. The course will also focus on race in America and its impact on those who identify as Black or African American. The course will examine "controversial" topics that are not typically discussed in a traditional school setting. Students will be free to express their thoughts and ideas based on specific facts presented throughout the course on a variety of different subjects. Critical thinking, debate, discussion, and analysis are critical to success in this course.

This course is for mature, adult students. As mentioned earlier we will be examining and discussing many controversial topics. Much of what you will learn in this class will come from your own research in the assignments that you complete. If you are not mature enough to handle a course like this, please feel free to drop out. Thank You!!!

There are no tests in the course. There are no right or wrong answers. Tests require right or wrong answers to be graded. That is not what I wanted. I wanted students to think freely, and outside the box. They had assignments (you'll get a sample of them later). The only wrong answer is an answer you, the student, got from someone else. All honest and thought-out answers with evidence to support them would get full credit for the student. Also, students would be required to explain their stance on a topic, and I would require them to critique it or find flaws in their logic. It was different. Critical thinking is hard. My students would not only be forced to think, but think critically. For a student to join the course in the future, they had to be vetted first. I had to meet them and find out their interest in the course. Most high school students are not ready for a class of this magnitude. I also did not want the course to become a dumping ground for students looking for an easy grade. Especially a dumping ground for Black students because the course is about Black experiences. There are several Black students I would never consider for this course, and several White, Hispanic, or Asian students I would consider. It is about the character of the individual, not the race.

The 2021-2022 school year began that September. I'm teaching this new elective. I explained all this to the students at the time about the course. They seemed genuinely interested and excited. One student in the course that I knew who had advocated for me to teach "African American History and Literature" was happy to see me teaching the new course. I thanked her for thinking so highly of me (during my 19 years of teaching my students tended to think much more highly of my teaching methods than many of my colleagues or former superiors). I told the students that they were now part of something new and different and there could be hurdles moving forward. They didn't mind. They all bought in. I got tremendous support from the NAACP (National Association for the Advancement of Colored People) and the AAECF (African American Educational and Cultural Festival, Inc) organizations within my district. At first, they thought that I was teaching African American History, but when I explained the change in the course to them, they were very supportive. One of the parents of a student in the class would send me materials to use. Even the student's grandmother would contact me. The support from the Black community members who knew about the course was great. It made me feel confident. However, my district was diverse. I wanted the support of the ENTIRE community.

"The Black Experience in America for Secondary Education", or simply "The Black Experience in America" is a half-year elective course that began in the 2021-2022 school year. It was designed for juniors and seniors in high school. The course examines critical issues and experiences of the many so-called African/Black Americans. It is a course centered around critical thinking. There are no right or wrong answers. Students are challenged to question everything and to analyze their long-held beliefs. Students are required to look at topics relating to the experiences of Black/African Americans through different lenses and perspectives. Throughout the course, students in the class led debates and discussions. They even created PowerPoint presentations to help prove their point of view, and other students and the instructor (me) were allowed to challenge their point of view.

I acted as a facilitator of discussion and debate. My role was to introduce a topic, give a brief history of it, and encourage debate. My role was also to play devil's advocate. No matter what perspective students gave, I gave the opposite perspective and challenged their thought processes. It does not mean they are wrong, but they are forced to look at things differently AND critique their own way of thinking. It does not mean they have to change their perspective, just understand the flaws in their perspective. Throughout the course, students have changed their perspective on some things, and have kept it the same on others. Too bad more adults won't do the same. The students rarely knew my position on a topic or issue. They could guess, but they never really knew.

Just because I challenged a train of thought does not mean I disagreed with it. Just because I say something to play devil's advocate doesn't mean that I agree with the statement that I am making. This course is not for most people. I always wonder if most schools are ready for a course like this. This course is different. Many public-school teachers and administrators do not like to think outside the box. Most educators do not like to take risks. Therefore, most schools will not be interested in a course like this. School districts and educators are infamous for doing the same things over and over under a different name or title. In the end, nothing changes. When presented with something different, not just in title but in action, many schools are not interested. I'm thrilled that my school district was. This is why public education is in the state that it is currently in. The philosophy is more of the same, under a different name. "The Black Experience in America" isn't that. I applaud my school district for having the guts to think outside the box. They were willing to take a chance and do something that may have been controversial. Most schools won't do it. Prior to teaching the first year of the course, I contacted the NY State chancellor of the Board of Regents to tell him about the new course but got no interest or response. I understand most schools do not want critical thinking even if they say they do.

In this book, the reader will examine issues and topics that affect not only Black Americans, but all Americans. This course is not designed just for Black people. It is designed for all. It is a combination of the history of specific topics, different experiences, and mindsets of Black Americans regarding the topics as well as other groups as it relates to Black Americans. Also, current events, articles, and video clips associated with Black/African Americans were used in the course. The topics covered in this book are just a sample of the discussions and debates we had in this course, as well as the thoughts of high schoolers regarding certain topics pertaining to the experiences of Black/African Americans. You, the reader, will never know my stance on any of the topics discussed. You will hear multiple perspectives on each topic. My beliefs on each topic will not be revealed in any way, shape, or form. Just because I ask a question or make a statement does not mean that is what I believe. I am creating dialogue and trying to inspire discussion. Do not make the mistake of assuming you know my beliefs while reading this. Welcome to "The Black Experience in America for Secondary Education."

CHAPTER TWO

THE WORD BLACK

The title of this course will trigger reactions from people. It is one of the reasons I decided to change the name of the course from "African American History and Literature" to "The Black Experience in America." It stands out. When people look at the title of the course and the book, they will immediately make some type of assumption. I'm sure this is true about most books. However, the reaction in this case may be a little more sensitive because of three words. Black, Experience, and America. This book, much like the course, is designed for open-minded people. Some people will look at this book with an open mind, curious as to the contents of this book. Those are the types of people the course is trying to attract. Even open-minded people come to new information with past assumptions. Others will look at the book and immediately have an ignorant reaction to it, with no intention of trying to see the contents of it. They will just make ignorant responses to it. Those are the types of people I want to scare off. I think many Americans make assumptions, rather than trying to understand before making a judgment. Therefore as stated earlier, most students and even fewer adults are built for a course like this. It is designed for the few. If everyone thinks the way you do, you can't be intelligent. Intelligence is like wealth. Most people don't have it. If everyone had a million dollars, then a million dollars wouldn't have much value. I am not saying that I am intelligent; however, I'm trying to be. Most people don't even try, which is why the course is not for most people.

TRIGGER WORDS

When you link the words Black and America in a sentence, it stirs many different types of emotions. It gets attention. Why? Indeed, both words come with a level of controversy. Both are powerful. Both can be looked at positively or negatively. People most certainly will have an opinion. This is where the discussion starts. America means many different things to many different people. To some people, it means freedom. To others, oppression. To some, it is the greatest country on Earth. To others, it is a country without value. For some, it is a forward-thinking country. For others, it is a country in steep decline. What are my thoughts? You will never know. Many people will dissect

America at some point. There is plenty of analysis of America. There is another word, however, that doesn't get analyzed quite as much.

Another trigger word is the word "experience." When some people read the title of the course or the cover of this book, they will immediately get turned off. The Black EXPERIENCE in America? They'll immediately think that the contents of this book will center solely around negativity, or blaming "the White man" for something, or that Black Americans are all victims, etc. Close-minded people are the type of people I am trying to turn away. An open-minded person will understand that so-called Black Americans have many different experiences. Ignorant people automatically assume and believe that so-called Black Americans have all had the same experiences, all think the exact same way, and are all liberal Democrats who hate or denounce White people. Critical thinkers understand that the people in any given group have many different experiences and perspectives, and a book such as this one or a course such as the one that I teach looks to examine these multitudes of experiences. The word experience along with Black and America creates an instant reaction for most. Hence, why I changed the course name. I wanted to be different. Outside the box. Words are words in most cases. How you choose to look at the words will determine if you think they are positive or negative.

BLACK

One of the earliest lessons discussed was having my students analyze the word "Black." This topic created one of the earliest debates and discussions for my students. What is it? The most common answer is color. Let's start there. I posed this question to my students. When you see the color black, what do you think? Have you ever thought about it? Have you ever analyzed it? They all answered they had not. Why would they? It is just a color, isn't it?

I know what adjectives come to my mind when I think of the color black. You will never know. Before you continue reading, write down all the adjectives that come to mind when you think of the color black. What does the color black represent to you? A simple activity, but it may have an impact in relation to this course and life in general. Are the adjectives you came up with your own thoughts? To some, it may represent beauty. To others, death. Some may say strength. Others may say it is ugly. Still, others may say it is mysterious. Others may say it's sexy. If you ask most people to list adjectives of the color black, you will almost certainly get different responses. However, that doesn't change the fact that most people subconsciously look at the color black in the same way. My students had different responses when it came to the color black and their interpretation of it. Some saw it as strong, others as beautiful. I asked them how they felt society viewed the color black. Their responses were pretty much in agreement, with answers ranging from depressing to sad. One student pointed out that for some reason society has associated the color black with death, which they explained is a popular color worn at funerals.

I asked the class, "Why do brides usually wear white in our society?" Now, if I asked people to list adjectives describing the color white or asked them what the color white means to them, you might get several different answers. If that is the case, why do brides almost always wear white at weddings? Of course, there are plenty of exceptions, but the class agreed that most women in America wear white to weddings. In fact, all the girls in the class said that they expected to wear white to their weddings. A woman may think that pink is the most beautiful color in the world. However, on her wedding day, she will still wear white. If she thinks that pink is the most beautiful color in the world, why wouldn't she wear pink? Why is it that most women on their wedding day wear white even though most women would rank different colors as their favorite? How many women would say that white is their favorite color? I posed these questions to the class, and they couldn't answer. They believed it made no sense.

I've never done a poll, but I am sure women universally would not say that white is their favorite color. So why do women insist on wearing a white dress on their wedding day? I asked the class if it could be the effect of indoctrination, or is it just tradition and traditions do not necessarily mean indoctrination. If a woman wore a black wedding dress, would people think of that as odd? What do you think? If you believe so, why would people think it is odd? It is just a color, isn't it? It could be the bride's favorite color. She may feel she looks better in black than in white. Why would people possibly look at it as odd? I asked 10 female students in one of my classes what their favorite color was. They all had different answers. Not one of them said white. I asked them what color they believed they looked best in. Again, multiple different answers, and again not one of them said white. I asked them what color they will wear at their wedding and nine out of 10 of them said, without thinking, white. One girl said black. The other nine girls who said white said they were going to wear white because of "tradition."

When I asked them why they wouldn't wear their best color at one of the greatest events of their life, they thought about it and said it didn't make sense to wear white. They began to realize that it was possible they were indoctrinated. If women all have different favorite colors or have different colors they feel comfortable wearing or feel they look great in, why do they all for the most part automatically go with a white dress? When we go to weddings, shouldn't we see brides in multiple different colored dresses? The common answer is, "It is tradition." If your answer starts with tradition, couldn't one argue that is the essence of indoctrination? If you answer that you believe in something for a different purpose and provide some evidence, that is at least some level of thinking. I'm sure more women today in America are wearing different colored dresses on their wedding day, but white still seems to be the dominant color of choice.

How many women planning to get married in white think outside the box? If they are doing it because of tradition, or societal pressure, then could critical thinking possibly have factored into their decisions? Most will respond that wearing a white dress represents the purity of the bride, as a couple of my students pointed out. In modern times, how many women walking down the aisle are actually "pure" in the intended meaning of why brides traditionally wear a white dress? Some students jokingly said that no bride is completely "pure" currently when walking down the aisle. No judgments, but if the dress is to represent purity, and a woman is not "pure" according to the tradition, isn't continuing to wear a white dress a sign of indoctrination? Of course, someone reading this will assume I have an issue with a woman wearing a white dress at her wedding. Let me remind you that over the course of this book, you will never know my stance on a subject.

I can argue against my own beliefs. That is the essence of the course. Looking at commonly held beliefs, analyzing them, and looking from a different perspective. No right or wrong answers. Most people cannot handle it. These questions were posed to the class.

Here's an activity. Listed below are words from a standard dictionary that start with the word BLACK. For each word, I had my students analyze the word. Feel free to do the same and either in your mind or on a sheet of paper indicate whether the word is positive or negative. If you don't know the definition, feel free to look it up to see if it is positive or negative.

ARE THESE WORDS POSITIVE OR NEGATIVE?

BLACK MARKET

BLACKLIST

BLACK EYE

BLACKOUT

BLACK MOOD

BLACK MAGIC

BLACK DEATH

BLACK PLAGUE

BLACK SHEEP

BLACK HAND

BLACK MAIL

BLACKBALL

BLACK MARK

BLACK CAT

BLACK COMEDY

The entire class believed that each of these words had a negative connotation. Are there any words that start with the word "black" that are positive? One student came up with black Friday, the day after Thanksgiving when stores have massive discounts on products. That was the only positive example of the word "black" that they came up with. Now let's do another activity. You will see a list of words, again beginning with the word "black." I had my students do another activity. This time, go through the words quickly and saying each word out loud with a rapid-fire response, indicate whether the word is positive or negative:

BLACK MARKET

BLACKLIST

BLACK EYE

BLACKOUT

BLACK MOOD

BLACK MAGIC

BLACK DEATH

BLACK PLAGUE

BLACK SHEEP

BLACK HAND

BLACK MAIL

BLACK BALL

BLACK MARK

BLACK GUARD

BLACK CAT

BLACK COMEDY

BLACK PEOPLE

When you got to the last term on the list, how was your mind programmed? What response were you initially going to say when you saw Black people? Positive or Negative? Only you would know. You could lie to yourself, but again only you would know. All the students in the class began to say negative, and they caught themselves. They gasped. They even felt guilty. I told them not to. You may have said negative and said it proudly. You may have started to say negative, then forced your mind to say positive. Nobody would know but you. This activity just illustrates how easy it can sometimes be to program the mind. So what is it with the word black? Where did it get such a negative connotation, I asked my students. Nobody came out of the womb thinking the word or the color black was negative. It had to be taught somewhere. It would have to be indoctrinated, wouldn't it? As always in the course, when addressing or looking at an issue, I like to go to the dictionary. The reason for this is that the dictionary is as emotionless as it gets (not to say that dictionaries aren't written by people with emotions). If you ask multiple people, the definition of a word you will get multiple answers. Those answers will be drenched in emotion, and usually, they will go with a definition that suits them personally. The definitions you see in this book and that are given in the course are not MY definitions. What are the dictionary (Merriam-Webster) definitions of the word BLACK:

-dirty, soiled

-thoroughly sinister, or evil: Wicked

-indicative of condemnation or discredit

-connected with or invoking the supernatural, especially evil

-very sad, gloomy, or calamitous

-marked by the occurrence of disaster

-characterized by hostility or angry discontent: sullen

-distorted or darkened by anger

Again, people can interpret the word or color black in many ways. However, the indoctrinating principle is, in general, that the color black is no good. How do you think this may affect how so-called non-Black people view so-called Black people in America? More importantly, how do you think this may affect how so-called Black Americans view themselves and other so-called Black people in America? I've heard that people in Africa, where "Black" people come from, do not refer to themselves as "Black." Many identify themselves in other ways. An African man once told me that in his home country, if I asked him, "What do you consider yourself," the last thing he would say is Black. I asked him why he wouldn't say he was a Black man, and he responded that everyone in his country would then have to identify themselves as "Black." It wouldn't make sense. Many times in Africa, he explained, people recognize themselves by their tribe, not by a racial component. Here in America, it is Black and White.

Speaking of white, think of the color or word white. What adjectives or descriptions come to mind when you think of the color white? Write them down on a sheet of paper. Compare them to the list you had for black. Again, I'm sure different people in the course and reading this book will have different reactions. None of them are right or wrong. Just different perspectives. Again, let's look at the dictionary definition, which is emotionless. Remember, when people need a definition of a word, they usually refer to a dictionary. These definitions of the word/color white are from the Merriam-Webster dictionary. These are NOT my definitions:

-free from spot or blemish

-free from moral impurity: INNOCENT (WHITE HEART)

-not intended to cause harm (white lie; white magic)

-favorable, fortunate (white days)

-passionate

-marked by the presence of snow (white Christmas)

What does this tell you about the color or the word white? How does it compare to the textbook definitions of black? Does anything stand out to you? Some of the definitions are considered old or archaic but the fact remains that these definitions were used for years. The students pointed out the clear differences between the two words. They admitted they had never analyzed the definitions of the two words, and they found this somewhat surprising. How do the definitions of white affect how White people are perceived, I asked them. A few students responded that they believed it subconsciously helped lead to racial stereotypes here in America and had a positive effect on White Americans and a negative effect on Black/African Americans. Individuals can look at things differently on a micro level. Societies on a macro level can look at things more similarly. I asked, "Is it possible that the words white and black are neither positive nor negative?" They are neither good nor bad. Are they just words that, depending on how you use them, can be good or bad? Just like any tool. Depends on how you use it, or how you interpret its use. If I use a hammer to hang a picture on my wall, that is much different than if I use a hammer to assault another person. A gun can murder an innocent, random person, or can be used to save my life. If we look at how the words/colors are typically used or looked at in America, how are they being used? With these definitions, is it possible that identifying as or being identified as a "Black" man could have a negative impact on my life in America if these are the definitions that have been accepted for the word or color black? Reread the question. I did not ask if these definitions of black have had a negative impact on my life as a "Black" man. You don't know me, or my situation so how could you possibly know? I asked if it were simply POSSIBLE. Is it possible that these interpretations on a macro level of our nation since the dawn of the United States of America could have had a negative impact on so-called "Black people" in America? I didn't ask if it did have a negative impact; I asked if it were possible.

Many times, white is seen in opposition to black, and black is seen in opposition to white. Someone once pointed out to me that babies born in a hospital are always wrapped in white cloth. Newborns and white signaling birth, the start of something new. At funerals we are taught to wear black, representing death and the end. Some people will see this as trivial. However, others will not. There are no right or wrong answers. Just observations and analysis. The representation of colors to YOU might not mean as much as to another person. So, let's pretend color does not matter. OK, great.

Growing up in the 1980s and 1990s color mattered to the crips and bloods gangs. Their rivalry was partly based on "color." In fact, one movie in the 1980s was literally called "Colors." The Ku Klux Klan wore and continues to wear "white" sheets. Executioners for centuries wore black robes. Just a coincidence? And while we are at it, since color doesn't matter, let's change the color of the White House to black. Hey, since it doesn't matter, why not? Let's change it up every few years. I'm sure that would be OK in a nation that doesn't see or doesn't think color is that meaningful. I asked the class if we repainted the White House black, what would the response be here in America? They all believed it would not go over well in this country. I asked why, and a student said because of tradition, and that in their opinion, black would not be accepted as the right color. One student pointed out that they have never seen an all-black building, and that could be a reason as well.

One student acknowledged that It's amazing how many Americans will claim they "don't see color" but will somehow wear black to every funeral or white for their wedding dress every single time. The student pointed out that some people will say they are color blind. If you didn't see color, shouldn't your color schemes be different for all these events? Or they will tell you they don't see skin color. OK, try this the next time someone says that to you. Ask them what race you are. If they say Black or White and they are correct, simply remind them they just said they don't see skin color, so it must've been a lucky guess. The point is, as much as you believe color doesn't matter, is it possible that it matters more than you think or give it credit for? Is it possible that white and black as defined here in America as being in constant opposition to each other could be a reason why so-called White and so-called Black people here have a history of tension and opposition as well? Could it be how we interpret the colors and how we label ourselves? I'm not saying yes or no. Just an analysis. I am asking you, the reader, as I asked my students. Again, there are no right or wrong answers as I mentioned to the class.

In the high school where I teach, a common term or slang that students use is "blackin." Not sure if you've heard of it before. Basically, the term is used to describe a student or person who has completely lost their mind and had become disruptive or was ready to get into a fight or altercation. The students would, for example, come into my classroom and say "so and so was blackin in the cafeteria." I immediately knew that they were doing something negative and were probably being aggressive and ready to throw down. It was a common term. One day, I heard the term being used and I asked the group of students using the word, "Why did you refer to the person's actions as blackin?" So, you are aware as the reader, the term did not just apply to Black students. It was used to apply to any student or teacher or for that matter any person in general who was exhibiting an unruly or aggressive demeanor or behavior. The students didn't know what I meant. I rephrased and asked, "Why is the term blackin a representation of someone being aggressive and unruly?" They didn't have a solid answer other than to explain that it meant that the person "blacked out" and lost their mind (again, another negative use of the word black). I then responded, "OK, so if blackin means that you have lost your mind, causing you to be aggressive and loud, does whitein mean I am studying and doing my homework and acting in a civil respectful manner?"

The students laughed and said yes it could. I got that idea from another teacher in my building who previously had brought it up to his students. Why does the word or color black almost always have to be associated with negativity? Again, could this affect how non-Black Americans view Black Americans, or more importantly, how Black Americans view other Black Americans? At the time of this writing, most Black murders are at the hands of another Black person. Most violence perpetrated against Black Americans is done by other Black Americans.

Could a possible reason start in the mind with how Black Americans look at each other, simply starting with the word or color black? Could Black Americans view each other as "lesser than" because the mind has been programmed that Black is less than? I'm not saying that's the reason; just posing a question to ponder. One of the reasons "The Black Experience in America" has its name is to try to get people, especially students, to look outside the box when examining the color or word black and the experiences that go with it for so-called Black Americans. While processing all this and how it may or may not have affected the experiences of Black Americans, let me leave something else for you to ponder. What if I told you I have no idea who Black Americans are? Do you?

Questions To Consider/Answer:

How might people's interpretation of color affect how they view people? Do you believe this has any effect at all on how we as a society, and you as a person, treat others?

What do you think of the color black? How would you describe the color?

How do you view so-called Black Americans? Does color have any impact on how you view them, no matter how small the impact?

Do you know who so-called Black Americans are? How would you describe them? Is it solely based on the color of their skin?

CHAPTER THREE
"BLACK" VS. "AFRICAN AMERICAN"

One of the discussions we had in the course was about Black and/or African Americans. Do you know who Black Americans are? Do you know who African Americans are? Are they the same? Are they different? Are you completely confused? At first, my students thought for sure they knew this answer, but once challenged they had to rethink their position. If you are confused, or after years of living in this country, you are perplexed on how to answer those questions, it is not your fault. You are beginning to think critically, and you may be in your mind trying to undo years of possible indoctrination. Most people fail to realize that confusion can be a good thing because it is a sign you're not only thinking, but you are also realizing there is more than one way to look at something. Earlier I stated that I am a "Black" man. Now while I am certain that I am a man, what if I told you that I am not certain that I am Black? (I didn't say I wasn't certain I am Black, but it is possible. I'm simply posing the same question that I posed to my students.)

I've had White people ask me what I prefer to be called. The class however, including the students who were not Black, never had a person ask them what they preferred to be called. Many times, they whisper the question as if they are afraid they are going to insult me somehow. It's not their fault. It's confusing. There have been multiple changes in racial designations as well over the years, so I don't blame them. Not to mention that in this country the word black tends to have a negative connotation, and many Americans seem to think of Africa as completely poor and destitute so the fear of offending me by linking me to the color black, or to the perception of a poor, struggling Africa may subconsciously make them nervous. Something so simple that you have identified with all your life can be challenged with one simple question or observation. Are people Black, or are they African American? Are they both? Or are they neither?

I did an activity with the students. I showed them a picture of Elon Musk and a picture of myself. If you showed 10 American adults or high school students my picture and a picture of Elon Musk and asked all 10 which of the two of us was African American, like my students, all 10 without thought would say I am African American. It's obvious, right? Elon Musk isn't African American, he is White. That was according to my students ... at first. Elon Musk was born in South Africa, and he has American citizenship. Being that he was born on the continent of Africa, and he also has American citizenship, why is HE not considered African American? It catches people off guard. The most common response is that he isn't Black. Why is African American synonymous with Black? Who created that standard? Is this right? Why can't he be White and African American? To show you how deep the indoctrination goes, I have never been to the continent of Africa. Elon Musk was born there. He has American citizenship, as do I. Why can he be considered an American, but I am an African American? Truth be told, I've been to Europe twice in my life, but I have never been to Africa. If it would be absurd to call me a European American just because I have American citizenship and I've been to Europe twice, would it not be even more absurd to call me African American being that I have never set foot on or been to the continent of Africa? Where do these terms come from? How am I supposed to identify myself in America? And why is it necessary? Let's take a deeper look.

AFRICAN AMERICAN

Let's start with the classification of African American. This was the next activity for the class. Let's assume I have no idea what or who an African American is. Let's start with dictionary definitions. We looked it up together as a class online from multiple dictionaries:

African American

-an American whose ancestors were born in Africa (Vocabulary.com)

-a person from America who is a member of a race of dark skin, originally from Africa (Oxford)

-Black people living in the United States who are descended from families that originally came from Africa (Collins Dictionary)

-an American of African, especially of Black African, descent (Merriam-Webster)

OK, got it. I have a few questions. The first definition says an American whose ancestors were born in Africa. If a White American's grandparents were born in Africa, as well as their parents, would that make them African American?

Second definition: A person from America who is a member of a race of dark skin, originally from Africa. OK, but now who determines what "dark" skin is? Am I dark-skinned? What is considered "dark skin?" Are people from Morocco, which is in northern Africa, dark-skinned? Do we call Moroccans African Americans? Still confused.

Third definition: Black people living in the United States who are descended from families that originally came from Africa

Fourth Definition: An American of African, especially of Black African, descent

According to the third and fourth definitions, color is the dominant determinant of an African American. If most people encounter a "Black" man or woman from Africa who is not an American citizen, why do they generally refer to them as African American? They aren't American. They will still classify all Black people in the exact same way, as African American. Are you confused? If so, you may be slowly undoing years of indoctrination.

The term "African American" started being used widely in 1988, even though the term was used before that year, just not as often as it is seen today. It started being used to refer to Americans of Black African descent. The roots of the term can be traced way back to the 1800s. Many African immigrants and many of their descendants may call themselves African Americans. There also may be Africans who are American but do not identify as African American. Many people who consider themselves African American support the term because they feel it gives them a cultural and geographic identity of their own in America(like Irish Americans who identify with Ireland, or Chinese Americans who identify with China). My family comes from the island of Barbados. Shouldn't I refer to myself as a Barbadian American (or Bajan American)? I've been to Barbados and seen where my family comes from. I've never been to Africa, nor could I tell you when in Africa my origins date to. What about Aboriginal Australians? Would they classify as African American if they moved to America permanently? Many others do not support the term, as they feel it makes them seem foreign in the United States, a country they, as well as their ancestors, helped to build. Those who are against the term argue that

White Americans are just called Americans, but Americans of darker skin tones are called African Americans as if they are second-rate Americans. The phrase European American is not used, so why use the term African American? White or Black, if you are born here, you are an American. Simple. Why separate? Some students believed that you needed to separate people in America because it is such a diverse nation and makes it easier to identify people. I asked them if this was beneficial for America, and they struggled to answer. Two students agreed that no matter what, there will always be division in America, so whether separated by "race," wealth, political alliance, or any other metric, America is a country designed to be divided.

One way some people show or have shown their hatred of, or practice discrimination toward, so-called African Americans is to yell at them to "Go Back To Africa." The students were all familiar with this phrase, though none of the Black students ever had it said to them. Where would a racist or a person practicing discrimination get such a ridiculous phrase to spew at so-called African Americans? Could it be because we look at certain groups of people in this country as African Americans? Maybe. The class seemed to think so. Let's dissect that hateful phrase. If a White man said to me or told me to "Go Back to Africa," I would politely tell HIM to "Go Back To Africa." His response would probably be, "I ain't from Africa," to which my response would be, again politely, "neither am I." Then he would have to think because if he had any sense or intelligence, he would probably start to realize how stupid he looks at that moment (people who start realizing they've been indoctrinated for most of their lives tend to feel a little silly when it has been exposed to them. As I always say, the more intelligent you become, the dumber you should feel).

His telling me to go back to a place that I have never been is just as ridiculous as me telling him to go back to a place he has never been. Yet he is using it toward me as an insult when it's not. How can I "Go Back to Africa?" I've never been there. Should I go back to Mongolia? I've never been there either. Why didn't he tell me to go back there? It would make more sense to tell me to go back to Europe since I've been there twice, but if he said that to me NOW that would make him look foolish, right? In fact, I've known White Americans who have traveled to Africa quite a few times, but that same hateful White man wouldn't yell at the White Americans I know who've been to Africa to go back there if they were trying to insult them. To some, it may still make sense. Others will question the logic of the insult. I asked the class if they had ever heard the phrase "Go Back to Europe" said to White Americans as an insult. None of them had. I asked them why they thought that was. One student remarked they believed that America accepts White people as Americans, and all other groups subconsciously as not as American. They pointed out that when they hear the term "real America" it is usually places where Black Americans are absent. No right or wrong answers, just observations.

BLACK AMERICANS (OR BLACK PEOPLE)

Next, the class analyzed Black Americans (Black people). Some would argue that I am not, or they are not African American, but they are Black, as am I. They would say that BLACK is the correct term. There was once a James Brown song called "Say It Loud I'm Black and I'm Proud." OK, so BLACK is the correct term. Got it. Black American is a more racialized classification of people, usually in a political context for people with dark brown complexions. Not all people considered "Black" have dark skin, and not all people with dark skin consider themselves "Black." The term "Black" people became extremely popular during the Civil Rights Movement in the 1960s. The goal was to unite all dark people with African ancestry. Also, the color black, as stated earlier, tends to stand out and is in your face. Revolutionary if you will, to some people. People with dark skin are not actually Black but have very dark brown skin.

When I compare my skin to the color black, I am nowhere near the same color or shade. So why am I classified as Black? Once again, confusion. Shouldn't I be singing "Say It Loud I'm Brown and I'm Proud?" Why are White people classified as White? Their skin is not actually white if you put the color of their skin next to the color white. What gives? Was this done to create division and opposition between the two groups? Maybe, maybe not. It doesn't really add up. Black is understood to describe race, while some think that the term African American refers to ethnicity. We will talk about race later in this book, but African American as an ethnicity refers to a group that has common national or cultural traditions.

I asked the class if it is fair to characterize all Black or African Americans as having a common national or cultural tradition. Aren't the experiences and cultures of all so-called Black/African Americans different? Where did the identification of Black come from if the people the term is meant to represent aren't actually "Black?" There are dark-skinned Indians who would never refer to themselves as Black. Some of them are darker than many so-called Black people. The obvious response is that the term is intended for dark people from Africa. OK, then what about dark-skinned Indians who were brought over to Africa by the British, let's say, and raised generations of families in Africa? If their offspring are dark, and they were born in Africa and moved to America, and attained American citizenship, are they African American? They should at least be able to call themselves Black, correct?

What about fair-skinned or light-skinned "Black" people? Are they Black? Is their skin dark brown enough to allow them to be classified as Black? If Black is the color that determines who is a Black American, then almost nobody can classify themselves as Black because all people come in various shades of brown. And once again, who determines what is the right shade to be considered Black? Some will argue it is completely up to the person to decide how they label themselves. That's great, but then can I label myself White? Most students felt it would be completely weird if I called myself a White man; however, if I am allowed to pick, why couldn't I call my race White? I asked if it would be weird because of the years of indoctrination that I was a Black man and not a White man, and they said that was the case. Someone will argue that is preposterous; my skin isn't white. Correct, it's not black either. They will then argue your family isn't from Europe. OK, but my family isn't from Africa either. They will then argue that my ancestry started in Black Africa. That's great, but according to scientists, the first humans were Black people who developed in southeastern Africa. If all humans on Earth can trace their origin to Blacks in southeastern Africa, wouldn't that make every single person in America technically African American no matter what color skin they have? Or is there a year or cutoff date to begin the separation of who is what based on the movement of certain people out of southeastern Africa? Please let me know the year. It is very hard to fit people into one box, isn't it? Or is it easier for society to group people in order to have a general identification of individuals? The students believed that these classifications were somewhat silly because they aren't always accurate. The class looked at things from a different perspective. A few students agreed that America has the idea of race too embedded in its society and as much sense as this may make, it will never change.

I asked the students whether broad categorizations of people as Black or White because they share a common culture is even accurate or fair, and if so, explain how? They all responded no. Should I be compared to all people identified as Black? Does that mean we are even similar? Couldn't that be dangerous? Also, the definition of Black people as the dictionary explains refers to any of the "dark-skinned" people from sub-Saharan Africa. Has anyone ever taken into consideration how large and diverse Africa is? By some estimates, there are upwards of 800 different languages in Africa. If we are tracing the term to dark-skinned people with a linkage to Africa, where in Africa? Are West Africans the same as Central and Eastern Africans? Are we only counting the Africans who were brought over as slaves to America from West Africa? My family was never brought to America as slaves. My parents were immigrants who moved to America from the Caribbean. Am I still African American? Am I Black? I had another student in the class who was of Caribbean descent. She said she considered herself Black, but the term African American was perfectly acceptable to her. The class was ok with either term, but they admitted it was because of years of hearing them interchangeably. They acknowledged both terms were indoctrinated into their heads since they were young. Two students, however, felt that changes needed to be made in the categorization of Black/African Americans because of the inaccuracies surrounding how the titles were being used.

The course called "The Black Experience in America" does not automatically mean that I endorse being called Black. It also doesn't mean that I don't want to be called Black. You will never know. In fact, what if there is another term that I would prefer to be called? The students love the name of the course. I even asked them at the beginning of the year if they thought there should be another name or a better title for the course since it was newly created, and the course centered around them. The entire class wanted to keep the name and they all said it sounded great. They admitted that it was much more captivating than "African American History."

PERSON OF COLOR/COLORED

This is confusing too. How is the term "person of color" defined? According to the Merriam-Webster dictionary, a person of color is defined as:

> *-a person whose skin pigmentation is other than and especially darker than what is considered characteristic of people typically defined as White*

OK, I got it. A person of color is a person who is not White. Would that mean that billions of people in the world, and all non-White people, fit into the same category? If I am a person of color, then why don't we refer to "White people" as people without color? Would that be offensive? If so, then how is calling me a person of color not insulting? "Colored" was a popular term for years. Today, it is considered an insult to call a Black or African American "colored." Why? Is it any different than calling me a person of color? If you think "colored" is fine, can we call White Americans "uncolored?" If you think "colored" is a slur, then do you also believe that the NAACP (the National Association for the Advancement of Colored People) should change its name? People of color or colored were not popular with the class.

NEGRO

The term Negro is another word that means Black in Spanish. Negro, like colored, was used for years, but now is considered offensive. Why exactly? If I identify as "Black," why is "Negro" such a bad thing? Why is it offensive? It just means black in Spanish. In fact, there was a time when the term Negro was considered polite, and BLACK was offensive. In today's world, it is the opposite. Why? What do these constant changes in classifications tell you? Does it indicate anything to you? In his "I Have a Dream Speech," The Reverend Dr. Martin Luther King Jr. used the term Negro several times. Should we change the word Negro in his speech to Black or African American or Person of Color? What if 150 years from now the term Black becomes offensive? Do we go back to Negro or colored? The whole discussion boils down to preference. If people within a specific category have so many options and opinions as to what they want to be called, couldn't that indicate that members of that grouping aren't as closely associated as we assume? Could it be that there are too many experiences to put people in a boxed category? The class did not like the term Negro at all. Speaking of preference....

BIRACIAL AMERICANS

There is a sizable population of people who are so-called mixed or biracial or even triracial. "Black" or "African Americans" who share multiple backgrounds have a choice to make. How do they classify themselves? Do they count as Black, African American, Negro, or Colored? If they have a Black and a White parent, are they a person of color still? Do they get to choose? Again, there are people who identify as "Black," even though their skin is not "dark," and there are those whose skin is "dark" who don't consider themselves Black, or African American. How are we to determine? Who decides? I am sure the actual person does, but will it be accepted by those around them? I've seen biracial people who claim they are not Black, but biracial people may be ostracized by members of the "Black community." Again, who gets to dictate all of this? Does this not prove that the experiences of Black Americans are extremely vast? The students believed that if one parent is Black and the other parent is White, then society identifies that person as Black. However, if one parent is Black and the other parent is Asian then it may be harder for society to determine their "race." One student pointed out that biracial Americans have it tough because both "races" want them to acknowledge that race as their race. I showed the class an article about a famous biracial actor of White/Black race saying she was black. I asked the class if they saw anything wrong with this. A couple of students did not like this and believed she should acknowledge her White heritage. Other students thought it was her choice to determine how she wants to identify herself.

Questions To Consider/Answer

Which term do you believe is proper? Why?

Whichever term you chose, explain why it is a flawed term.

CHAPTER FOUR

RACE: DOES IT EVEN EXIST?

WHAT IS RACE?

The next three topics in the curriculum led to the most discussion and debate in the class. We spent weeks analyzing and discussing them. You cannot talk about The Black Experience in America and not discuss race. Anyone who tries is delusional. In today's America many people freak out when the word "race" is brought up, especially around students. Some people feel race should never be discussed. Others claim not to notice race. That's odd because everything from applying for a driver's license to signing up for school to filling out a census to filing for a mortgage asks a person what "race" they are. Many Americans become uncomfortable when the word is mentioned. It's to the point where if I challenged one of my students to a race after school, some parents would accuse me of teaching "Critical Race Theory." Again, I have no connection to Critical Race Theory and I have never seen its actual curriculum and neither have 99% of the people who have an opinion about it.

This extreme fear of discussing "controversial" things in America is very unnerving. America is supposed to be the land of freedom of speech. People will even cite it as their First Amendment right. In reality, people only want you to speak freely when you are saying something they agree with. Americans also only want you to speak freely if you are saying something they feel comfortable with. This is very disturbing. This is one of the reasons many people are afraid to think critically. They know the moment they say something that is controversial, people will lose their minds. If you wanted to challenge the idea that America was a land of freedom of speech you could do so simply by mentioning or discussing the word race.

When I got to the topic of race in the course, I asked the students to tell me what race they were. They began to think before they answered. What they thought they had known all their lives they now began to question. They were now getting the idea of how the course worked. At this point, we were about two months into the course. They were finally seeing that things were not as simple as they had previously thought. They knew that no matter what they said, I would present a different perspective. The hesitation in their answers showed that they were now starting to think for themselves. It didn't mean that their answers would be wrong, but it meant that they were finally thinking critically, and they had to think before they spoke. Even though my students knew the answer to the question of what their race was they still had to take a second to think about it first. That is the essence of critical thinking.

One of my favorite sitcoms of all time is "Seinfeld." I watched it when I was a teenager, and I still watch it in reruns today. Most of my students had either heard of the show or were not too familiar with it. There was one episode that I mentioned to the class that had to do with what we would be discussing. It was season 9, episode 15, titled "The Wizard." I showed them a three-minute compilation of the episode. If you've never seen it, in this episode Elaine, the main female character, introduces her new boyfriend, Daryl Nelson to Jerry and George, two other main characters. When Daryl briefly excuses himself, Elaine asks the two what they think of Daryl, and Jerry is curious if she is asking about her dating a Black guy. Elaine is stunned. She is confused because she did not think Daryl was Black. It didn't matter to her whether he was Black or not, but her curiosity was now sparked as none of them could determine Daryl's race just by looking at him. They then become uncomfortable talking about race and move on.

Later in the episode, Elaine goes to Daryl's apartment. She tries to figure out his race using clues in his apartment but that only confuses her more. She buys him a piece of technology (a wizard) and tries to get him to fill out the warranty information, skipping right away to the part on race. Daryl asks if filling it out matters and Elaine tells him no, but they should fill it out anyway. Daryl then tells her to check Asian. Elaine looks confused and Daryl laughs, saying he just wants to confuse the warranty company. Elaine has lunch with George, asking him what she should do. George tells Elaine to just ask him, which she refuses to do. George again tells her they shouldn't be discussing this. Elaine explains to George that she has decided that they should just start going to Spanish restaurants as she doesn't know what type of food he may like.

Daryl and Elaine have lunch in a coffee shop and Daryl remarks that he still can't believe people have an issue with interracial couples after another couple seems to look at them strangely. Elaine is now convinced Daryl is Black. Toward the end of the episode Daryl and Elaine meet in the coffee shop once again and Daryl overhears Elaine telling the waitress her boyfriend is Black. A surprised Daryl responds that he isn't Black. Elaine remarks that Daryl earlier stated they were an interracial couple to which Daryl remarks that they are because Elaine is Spanish. Elaine asks why he would think she was Spanish to which Daryl remarks because she has curly hair, her last name is Benes and she kept taking him to Spanish restaurants. They then realize that they are both "White," accept it and decide to shop at The Gap (a stereotypically White clothing store based on the reaction on the show). This episode is actually a great example of how difficult the discussion of race can be in the United States. The students enjoyed the clip. Although most were not familiar with the show, they did see the humor in the confusion over people's race and identification.

Once again, when discussing a topic or issue, we first define the issue and take a brief historical look at the issue at hand. Now, race is a hard word to define. As a class we looked up the definition and we saw many. Here are some of the definitions that we found.

RACE

-any one of the groups that humans are often divided into based on physical traits regarded as common among people of shared ancestry (Merriam-Webster)

-the idea that the human species is divided into distinct groups on the basis of inherited physical and behavioral differences (Britannica)

-one of the main groups to which people are often considered to belong, based on physical characteristics that are perceived to share such as skin color, eye shape, etc. (Cambridge)

There were several others, but they were all similar. So, race is basically a grouping of people who are similar, right? Not so fast. If you and I look alike, then we must be of the same race. Obviously. What are the different racial groups, according to the United States Census Bureau? Using the website census.gov, the class looked.

Black or African American

White

American Indian or Alaska Native

Asian

Native Hawaiian or Other Pacific Islander

Some other race

Mistakenly some people think Hispanic is a race, but according to the Census Bureau, it is an ethnicity, not a race at the time of this writing.

I asked the class when they were children and they first started speaking, did anyone ask them what race they were? If they had, what would their response have been? Would they have known to say that they were Black or White? Or did someone tell them what race they were? Could that have been indoctrination? Were they allowed to challenge the concept of their race as they got older, or did they just accept their "race" as they were told? What about you, the reader?

Also, racial categories have changed throughout the years so how do we know they won't change again 100 years from now? How accurate are these "racial" classifications? Based on these "racial" groupings, we looked at the students in the course. We had five students who identified as Black or African American. Two of my students identified as Hispanic, and one student was Native American (or American Indian). When I pointed out to the two Hispanic students that according to the United States Census Bureau, being Hispanic was an ethnicity, not a race, one student said she was Black or Afro-Hispanic (her family was from the Dominican Republic), and the other girl said she had no idea how to classify her race.

She said in the school's system, they always labeled her as White. I asked her if she labeled or classified herself as White, and she said no. The confusion was just beginning. I also asked, "If Hispanic is not a race, why does the term Hispanic even exist?" One of the Hispanic students in the course didn't understand it either. If you are Black and your family comes from a Spanish-speaking country, doesn't that mean you are still part of the Black race? Why do we even need to add Hispanic to the mix? Wouldn't they just be Black or African American based on the definition? One student said it is probably because they speak Spanish. I then responded that Haitians speak Creole, and they are Black, but there is not a separate category for them. They would still check Black/African American. Why is there an emphasis on whether you speak Spanish? The student had no answer. A "Hispanic" person can pick White or Black "Hispanic", but couldn't they just pick White or Black and be done with it? Why bring ethnicity into the mix? I thought the Census Bureau was talking about race.

The class found it funny how some people in America try to act as though race is irrelevant in our society but everywhere you turn society wants to know your "race." One thing that was pointed out in class was the fact that White was a simple racial grouping, but Black had to be accompanied by African American, even though White was not accompanied by European American. My students pondered why the Census Bureau would have it labeled that way. If White was good enough, why wasn't Black? Who came up with this? I had no concrete answer. I had a belief as to why, but again my students aren't allowed to know what I think. Neither will you. Some said they believed it was done intentionally to make Blacks seem as if they are not as American as White Americans. Those are not my words; it was an observation made by some students. Either way, they were thinking for themselves.

Another observation the class made was about the Asian racial category. Again, based on the basic definitions of race, it is a grouping of people who share certain physical traits in common. Asia easily has over four billion people. Could four billion people seriously and realistically share common physical traits and characteristics? Do people in Sri Lanka have similar physical traits to people in North Korea? Do people in Pakistan have similar traits to people in Mongolia? What about people who live in Eastern Siberia? Are they White or Asian? If the entire continent of Asia is considered a racial group, then is the entire continent of Africa a racial group? Do northern Africans count as Black/African American?

As a class, we then began to break down and study the Black/African American "racial group" here in our country, and we analyzed the definitions we saw. There's a common joke that is told here in America when one Black person is confused with another. The response is "Do all Black people look alike?" Some people may use it and be offended if they are compared to another Black person, but many Black people use it as a joke, usually toward a member of another race. However, if we really break it down, according to the United States Census Bureau and the definitions we saw, all Black people DO look alike, which is why we are being grouped into the Black/African American racial group. Thinking about it now, it ISN'T a joke. It now makes a lot of sense why I might get confused with another Black person. Can I really get angry if a police officer arrests me by accident, having confused me with another Black person? After all, he or she was doing their job. According to the United States government, all Black people look alike based on the definition of race.

Could I even call a person a racist if they were to tell me that all Black people look alike? Ironically, if I were arrested or the police were actively searching for me, the first description they would have for me is a "Black" male. What if I identify as another race? After all, that is my legal option as an American, isn't it? Why not? If I can identify myself as another gender in today's America, would identifying myself as another race be any different? What if on the day the police try to arrest me, I feel like an Asian American? Originally, the cops were searching for a "Black male suspect." I'm not Black anymore, so they'd have to release me, right? Clearly, this wouldn't happen, but the belief that I get to pick my "race" may not be THAT accurate. It seems that my "race" was picked for me, much like my Hispanic student who didn't know what "race" she was, but in the school's system she was labeled "White." I asked the students if they picked their "race" when they were a child. They all said no. I asked them if they were ever given the opportunity, to which they replied no. The students pointed out that their "race" was determined for them, without them ever challenging the concept until this class. It really got them thinking. One student questioned if they were indoctrinated with the concept of race.

The next thing the class tried to examine is what the phrase "common physical traits" means. I asked the students what is a common physical trait of all people classified as "Black/African American?" What seemed like an easy question to answer before the course now was difficult for them. They began to debate it. To help guide them, I looked for basic requirements that might help them. I asked if there is a height requirement. Well obviously, no. There are tall and short Black/African Americans. One study I showed the class states that Africa is the most genetically diverse continent in the world (Nature.com). Also, Africa, according to some counts, has at least 1,000 different dialects and languages (Nationsonline.org). Would all these people be a part of the same race of African American here in the United States? If I moved to Africa and gave up my American citizenship, is my race still African American? Why wouldn't it be? Does my race change depending on where I live? A few students voiced how silly a lot of this can be. OK, well clearly the person must be dark-skinned to count, right? That didn't work well, because just sitting in the class I had students who were very "light-skinned" and students who were darker. This was pointed out by the students.

The Census Bureau didn't give or attach a skin color guide or a shade chart to their website, so basing it on skin color was nearly impossible. People will claim that race isn't about looks, it is about ancestry; however, that is not the case when a person first lays eyes on you. A stranger couldn't possibly know your ancestry but will quickly identify you by race. They then tried facial features. Black/African Americans have full lips, they said. How full do the lips have to be? So, Black Americans have fuller lips than others. Is there a lip guide? Some students said curly or "nappy" hair. Great!! How tight or curly or nappy does the hair have to be? They said broad noses. What is a broad nose? How broad does it have to be? It was getting harder and harder for them. The students tried to indicate that a Black person is a Black person, "you can just tell." I wasn't letting them off that easily. If you are going to group people together, there should be a criteria that is fairly accurate, shouldn't there? Is it fair to group me, a teacher with no criminal record, with a person who has a criminal record a mile long simply because we are both "Black?" Whenever statistics are done in America by race, that is how we are categorized. Couldn't this lead to stereotypes that are unfair to all "Black" people? And again, do ALL Black people look alike? If you say yes, you'll be labeled a racist. However, you would be going by some of the dictionary definitions that are given, so you are not wrong. So-called Black people come in all different shapes, colors, and sizes. I asked the class if all Black people look alike and jokingly, they said yes before acknowledging they thought that was ridiculous.

DOES RACE EXIST?

One of the definitions that the class analyzed started with "the idea." So, is race an idea? If you ask multiple people what race is, you will get multiple ideas. That is the essence of this course. Looking at different ideas and perspectives to think critically about the topic. The class read an article from Vox.com titled "11 Ways Race Isn't Real" written in 2014 by Jenee Desmond-Harris. This was to give them a different perspective on what they knew about race. Many people have heard of the Caucasoid, Mongoloid, and Negroid racial groupings. I guess as a "Black/African American" man, I belong to the Negroid grouping. The groupings are based on genetics and anthropology. I am an expert in neither the field of genetics nor anthropology. What classifies someone as a Negroid? The class examined common themes of a Negroid using a google search and here are some things that they saw:

-someone with dark skin

-coarse back, wooly hair

-wide nose

-thick lips

-extreme adaptability to heat

The last one we saw in our search was very interesting. Apparently Negroid or Black/African Americans are great in the heat. Now personally, I love the heat. I know plenty of Black/African American/Negroids who hate the heat and prefer the cold. Are they Negroid? Am I even allowed to use the term Negroid? From the research the class did, it seems that the term is obsolete. Very confusing. One student pointed out that race can't be based on how people behave. Not all "Black/African Americans" act the same, so how could you base them on social behavior?

With all of this, the class then decided to discuss if different races actually exist. If one of the definitions starts with, "it is an idea," then does that mean we are free not to believe in the idea of race? When

I asked the students to tell me their race at the beginning of the unit on race, they all told the class the race they believed themselves to be. They were simply regurgitating what they had been trained to believe their entire lives. At this point, they began to question things. I asked them why, when I asked them what race they were, none of them said "human?" As in the human race. They had no answer. They then began discussing whether humans are an actual race. I pointed out that it is literally called the "human race," so why wouldn't it be a race? They pointed out that people look vastly different so that is why there could be different races. I responded what if we aren't so different from each other, we just look different? Everyone in a family looks different but you wouldn't separate your mother and father from the children into different races, would you? Some will point out it is based on ancestry, but how far back in the ancestral line does one have to go? All humans developed in Africa. Do we ignore that when looking at ancestry? What if a White man were born in Africa in the 1800s? Could his great-grandchildren identify as African American if they were born in the United States? How far back are we to trace our ancestry? Students then began to ask what accounts for the differences between people that are genetic in nature.

Many people, as my students would point out, believe that "Black" people are better at specific sports than other races, such as football, basketball, boxing, etc. They said that Black people disproportionately being represented in these sports compared to the general population showed there is scientific evidence that race does indeed exist. Again, I am not telling my students what to think (indoctrination). I challenged them based on their statements. I am no scientist, nor do I try to be. I explained this to them. I asked them if the differences between different "races" or "groups" actually had nothing to do with race, but more to do with geography and culture as opposed to the idea of different races. They couldn't understand how. Black people were faster, could jump higher, and excelled in sports. That must be based on race. I wanted to show them another perspective.

I pointed out that most so-called Black/African Americans in the Americas are from Western Africa. There is no doubt that Black Americans who are direct descendants of West Africans excel at sports such as football, basketball, baseball, boxing, and wrestling. Those from the Caribbean who are "Black" excel at track. Black athletes tend to be extremely strong and fast. For example, Black athletes make up about 70-75% of the National Basketball Association, while as of 2021 "Blacks" make up only 13-14% of the current population of the United States. Clearly, there is a disparity. The common belief among the students was clearly, it's due to race. Black athletes, they contended, are stronger, faster, and better athletically because they are Black. Simple. I wanted to point something else out, however. Could it have more to do with geography and not race? My students were confused. I explained to them that "Black" dominance in these fields could be due to the geographic factors that forced West Africans and their recent descendants to develop certain genetic adaptations to survive in that region.

As our earliest ancestors moved out of Africa to other areas, they had to develop adaptations to live in their respective environments. So instead of it being a "racial" reason, could it be due more to the geography of where they settled? I showed the class an article from The New York Times called "Nobody Does It Better" by Jim Holt about West Africans and their descendants. West Africans and their descendants had a higher proportion of fast-twitch muscle fibers than slow-twitch muscle fibers than other "racial" groups. Fast-twitch muscle fibers were useful in helping people in West Africa defend against malaria. Fast-twitch muscle fibers are great for strength and explosive abilities (for sports such as track, football, basketball, etc.). West Africans had to develop fast-twitch muscle fibers to help them settle and stay in that region of Africa for generations. It was an adaptation.

I also heard that the same defense against malaria also disproportionately created the sickle-cell disease that is more prevalent in West Africans and their descendants. East Africans, according to the theory, have better slow-twitch muscle fibers, which are an adaptation to their environment. Slow-twitch muscle fibers are beneficial for endurance, which is one of the reasons East Africans excel at marathons. If malaria was prevalent in Eastern Europe, let's say, is it possible Eastern Europeans and their descendants in America would dominate sports such as track, football, etc.? My students thought about it. If Asian people had settled and stayed in Western Africa for generations (obviously they wouldn't then be considered Asian, but just go with the flow), is it possible they would have developed certain adaptations that would allow them to dominate these sports? I don't know the answer. I wanted to open their minds to something they may have never been exposed to. I encouraged them to do the research. Is it possible that Black dominance of these sports would be more about geography than being a separate race? They acknowledged that it was possible, but they wanted to research more about this. They had never heard of this before and were intrigued by it.

I asked my students if East African descendants born in America were African American or Black as well. They responded that, according to the census and common belief, they would have to be. I asked them why they didn't also dominate in the sports mentioned before. They didn't know. I pointed out that East Africans and their direct descendants dominated in marathon running. Could it be because of the area in East Africa their ancestors settled? Did they adapt to their environment? How is it possible that two different groups in the "same race" have so many differences? Why aren't West and East Africans divided into two different races? I've heard people argue that West and East Africans and their direct descendants do not even look alike. The Maasai Tribe in Africa are some of the tallest people in the world. However, the Pygmy tribe are some of the smallest. Yet in America, both would be Black/African American. I asked, "How similar are their physical traits?" The students said they aren't really. However, in America, they would still all be called "Black/African American" if they were born in this country.

Could another major difference between "races" have more to do with culture than actual race? Could the lifestyle and foods that are eaten play more of a role among people than the actual "race" they are? Within the many different tribes of Africa is it possible they look vastly different because of culture? Could one "race" excel over another in certain fields due to the way of life of that group instead of a major difference in so-called race? The class had a very good debate about this. We discussed culture later in the class. Three of my students believed culture and environment had much more to do with the development of people than their race.

COLORISM

The class also had a conversation about colorism within the "Black" community or "Black" racial group. Even though the class knew what it was, I always wanted to use a generally accepted definition of the word that we could work from. The definition of colorism from our Google search:

> -*a form of racial discrimination based on the shade of an individual's skin tone (Dictionary.com)*
>
> -*prejudice or discrimination within a racial or ethnic group favoring people with lighter skin or people with darker skin (Merriam-Webster)*

There are differences within virtually every "racial" group. Colorism is an example of this. In the class, I had "Black" students of different shades. Again, race is supposed to group people together based on common traits and characteristics, mostly physical. If that is the case, why would colorism exist? You have so-called Black people who are so-called light-skinned and so-called dark-skinned people who are dark-skinned. Why are they not in two separate races? I asked my students these questions. They wondered aloud what the criteria was for being in a certain group since the definitions that we saw were not very consistent.

One student pointed out that it may still have to do with the ancestral breakdown that you are considered to be of the Black/African American race if your ancestors came from Africa. Unless you did a DNA test, how do you know where every single person's ancestry came from? It is more of a guess. You could have ancestors from many different backgrounds. Why pick one over the other? Colorism has been a major issue among the Black racial group. Black people have always discussed how, way back even to slavery, there was a separation between lighter and darker Blacks/African Americans. Even in dating, many people have a preference of what type of person they want to end up with. Some like the lighter shade, and some like the darker shade. I discussed this with my students. If Black people were so similar in physical traits, how could there be so many preferences among Black people in desirable looks? They responded that they have seen colorism in their personal lives, so it was nothing new to them. Some students admitted they were the victims of it among their friends and families. They also acknowledged that they too have done it as well. Not all the students but a couple. They gave the example of making fun of other Black people for being too "dark." They also acknowledged that it has been an issue among Black people. They were familiar with the term.

THE BLACK COMMUNITY

There is a phrase or term called "The Black Community" that is synonymous with the Black racial group. During our discussion on race, I asked the students to explain what is or who is a part of The Black Community. They thought about it. By this point in the course, they were learning to think before they spoke because they knew that whatever beliefs they had would be challenged. They answered that it should be people who consider themselves Black. I asked if a "dark-skinned White" person could be a part of the Black community. Some argued no, and some weren't sure how to answer. I then asked, why not? Earlier you stated that if the person considers themselves to be Black, then they could be part of the Black community. They then said that the person had to be Black, and that takes us back to the beginning. I also mentioned to my students that among Black people, there has always been an issue where some Black people will say that another Black person "isn't really Black." The students had heard that before. I asked, "What does that mean?"

In the discussion, some of the students explained that it means that the Black person is acting non-Black (usually meaning "acting White"). It could also mean that they weren't into "Black culture." I pointed out that, in the early 1990s, many in the so-called Black community considered former President Bill Clinton to be America's first Black president even though he was a White man. Clearly, it was a joke, but why would they say this? He was perceived to be smooth, cool, and a ladies man. Many Blacks were willing to let him into the Black community, while others would say certain other Black Americans weren't really Black, they were really White. To add insult, they would say some Black people were "White people in Black face." This comment has been pervasive about Black Republicans among many Black Americans. Why are they not considered part of the Black community by many Black

Americans when the definitions that were given earlier clearly state that they would be? Who is determining what race a person belongs to?

WHAT IS THE POINT OF "RACE" IN THE FIRST PLACE?

I asked my students, "What is the point of race in the first place?" The basic answer given was to help identify people. I jokingly responded, "isn't that why you have a name?" They answered that race may be needed to assess how to help certain groups. As I had pointed out to them, even within certain groups many subgroups exist, so how could you possibly help everyone? Also, if you are using race to identify people, what if people are identified inaccurately? If the definition of race is based on an idea, what if having different races is just a bad idea? Who determines these ideas? I pointed out that Middle Eastern and North African people are considered to be White. The class vehemently disagreed with this.

I have a friend from the Middle East who does not consider himself to be White. Whose idea am I supposed to follow? Also, whenever terrorists from the Middle East attack the United States, they are never looked at as "White terrorists." They are always labeled as Muslim, Arab, or Middle Eastern. If someone referred to them as "White" terrorists, the response you probably would get is they are not White. Very confusing. Also, people can change their race with the Census Bureau. If I can change my race, then what is the point of keeping tabs on a person's race? How do we know if the statistics kept on different "races" are even accurate?

If a person can pick their race, can a White student apply for a scholarship meant for Black/African American students? Why not? Who is to tell them that they are not Black/African American if the individual is allowed to pick? I asked the class about Albinos. Why are they considered Black? The students responded they have Black features. My response was they lack much melanin, like White people. Why aren't they White? And once again, what are Black features? Round and round we go. The class theorized that the concept or idea of different races really took off during colonization to justify the capture and enslavement and mistreatment of certain groups. Just as nobody looks at a bull pulling a plow and feels bad, the class believed that it is possible if people viewed certain races as inferior, it might justify their mistreatment. Many of the students pointed to the American enslavement of Blacks as an example. Is this right or wrong? Just their thought process after our discussion. Race is hard to define. And as you'll see in the next chapter, a word associated with race is even harder to define and process.

Questions To Consider/Answer

Describe what race is in your own words. Do you believe all humans need to be or should be categorized by a particular "race?" Why or why not?

Is it possible that the classification of Blacks into "the Black racial category" is harmful to Black Americans? Why? Is there a possibility it can be helpful?

What race do you consider yourself to be? Explain why

CHAPTER FIVE

RACISM: IS IT ACTUALLY HARMFUL?

KEEP AN OPEN MIND

Here is another word that is an immediate trigger for everyone in America. RACISM. Before we delve into this, we may be able to acknowledge that people have mixed feelings about this topic. Once again in a nation of "free speech," when people begin to "speak freely" on a topic, many others get upset and tell them to stop. Many people feel that if they ignore the topic, it will make things better. Others believe that the more you discuss racism, the better things will become in our society. Who is right? Who is wrong? What I can tell you is that, in the United States of America, when discussing The Black Experience, there is no way you ignore the topic of racism. If you ignore it, then you are not talking authentically about The Black Experience in America. So, one of the major topics of the course centers around racism.

During the semester, our class spent the most time talking about this topic. It was a lot to digest. At the end of this unit, some of my students changed their minds about how they had seen things from the start of the unit. I did not force them to change their minds or keep their current mindset. Remember, whatever they said, my job was to challenge them, to inspire them to think and look at things from a different perspective. What they think in the end is completely up to them. If you ask them, most Black people will tell you that we need to end racism in America. When we started the unit, my students believed we needed to end racism. I asked, "How do we end it?" Nobody had an answer. It was dead silence. As you continue reading, please keep an open mind. It doesn't mean you need to change your mind, but it is possible you may answer with an indoctrinated answer. Again, as with all topics in this course, we are looking at things from different perspectives as it relates to The Black Experience in America. It is easier for young adults to keep an open mind than older adults. Try to keep an open mind. If you can't, then please skip this chapter. Here we go ….

WHAT IS RACISM?

Let's start with this. Are people born inherently racist? Is racism taught (indoctrination)? I'll ask you what I asked my students at the very beginning of this unit. ARE YOU A RACIST? Answer the question on a sheet of paper or in your head. I asked my students the same question. Can you guess what their responses were? If you said they responded with no, or absolutely not, you would be correct. Next, I asked them if they thought I was a racist? They said no, not you, Mr. Boyce. I asked the class if they ever had a racist encounter with anybody in their lives? Every student told a story of someone they know saying something racist to them. It was all disturbing. I asked them if they had told anyone else. One student said she told her parents. The rest said they hadn't told anyone, and this was the first time they were speaking about it. I had to sit down as I discussed this with them.

I am sure they are not the only students who have experienced racism. They said that they felt if they told anyone, it would have fallen on deaf ears. That is a problem. I wonder how many other students feel this way as well. One of the beautiful things about this course is that students are allowed to express themselves freely. Most to no other courses that they had taken up until that point allowed them to do so. I was honored that they placed that much trust in me to tell me what they told me.

I asked if they believed there are racist teachers who teach in our district. They said absolutely, without a doubt. They said racist teachers were wrong and should be fired and that all schools have racist teachers to some degree. I said OK, got it. I asked again if they thought I was a racist teacher. They again responded no way. I asked them again if they were racist. They said no, not at all. I will ask you the reader, once again, are you a racist? I then asked the students what if I, Mr. Boyce, admitted to being a racist. They looked at me, confused.

I said yes, I am a racist. What do you think now? They were still confused. Mr. Boyce, you are not a racist. You're nice to everyone was the class consensus. I replied, "So what?" I am still a racist. They were perplexed. I even told them that I am one of the most racist teachers in the building (clearly for those of you who may not have figured it out yet, I am playing devil's advocate. I might not be a racist or I might be a racist, you do not know me. Don't decide until you finish the chapter). I then asked them on a sheet of paper to define the word racism. You, as the reader, do the same. Define the word racism on a sheet of paper WITHOUT the use of a dictionary.

Black Americans, as with most other groups in America, believe that we need to "end racism," "fight racism," or "destroy racism." Do most Americans know the definition of racism? How can we end, fight, or destroy something we don't know? People define racism with their own idea of racism and to their own liking. I asked the class, "Is it possible that people define racism in a way that makes THEM themselves NOT racist?" Do we know the definition of racism? Are our definitions of the words given to us (indoctrination) from someone else? How many people have thought about what racism really is? If I walked into a room of Black Americans and said racism is harmless, what is the big fuss, most in the room would probably look at me like I was insane. In fact, some might say I'm not Black (here we go again with the race thing). As we do in this course, before we go deeper into something, we look up and analyze the definition. And that's where we start.

If race is hard to define, racism is even harder. Now that you have written the definition of racism, let's look at the definition of racism given by standard dictionaries. Racism is defined as:

-a BELIEF that RACE is the primary determinant of human traits and capacities and that racial differences produce an inherent superiority of a particular race (Merriam-Webster)

-racism is the BELIEF that people of some races are inferior to others, and the behavior which is the result of this belief (Oxford)

-the BELIEF that humans may be divided into separate and exclusive biological entities called "races" (Britannica)

-a BELIEF or doctrine that inherent differences among various human racial groups determine cultural or individual achievement, usually involving the idea that one's own race is superior and has the right to dominate others or that a particular racial group is inferior to the others (Dictionary.com)

-policies, behaviors, rules that result in a continued unfair advantage to some people and unfair or harmful treatment of others based on race (Cambridge Dictionary)

There are many more definitions that I am sure we can find but in the interest of time we went with these definitions, as most definitions generally looked similar. One definition we saw on Google was *"Prejudice, discrimination or antagonism directed against a person or people on the basis of their membership in a particular racial group, typically one that is a minority."* We will look back at that definition a little later. I asked my students to compare their definitions of racism to the definitions we looked up. I will ask you to do the same. How does your definition of racism compare to the dictionary definitions above?

Almost all my students had pretty much the same definition, just worded differently. I'm sure if you ask a child or even look at your own definition, it may be similar. The most common definition my students gave me (and other adults when I asked them) was that racism was an "Extreme HATE or DISLIKE for another racial group" OR "When a person thinks that one group is beneath or inferior to another." What was your definition? If all these students have a similar definition (which they did), could that be indoctrination? I asked them if racism was bad. They said absolutely. I once again asked them if they were racist. They said absolutely not. And this is where things got interesting. Again, there are no right or wrong answers, just an analysis of things from a DIFFERENT perspective. Here goes …

IS RACISM HARMFUL?

Black Americans are constantly talking about fighting racism or ending racism. I asked my students if we should try to fight racism? Is fighting racism a worthy cause? They said yes, absolutely. I responded (again playing devil's advocate) that it is a waste of time, and we should not fight racism at all. They looked at me like I was crazy. They asked me what I meant. We analyzed the definitions of racism. When we read through, we looked for common themes. You, as the reader, do the same. One thing that is common to most definitions of racism is the word belief. I pointed out to my students that none of the definitions we looked at included the word *hate*. I asked them where they got the idea that racism was about hate, as many of them used the word hate in their definitions They really didn't know, other than they got the idea from their parents or school. I told them we are now going to look at things from a different perspective.

I asked the students if a belief is harmful. They said yes. I asked them to explain how. They said that a belief or the way you think can influence the way you act. I pointed out to them that an act is different from a belief, although I acknowledge that acts usually occur from a way of thinking first. We all may have different beliefs, or think certain things, but in many cases we do not act on those beliefs or thoughts. Are beliefs really that dangerous if we don't act on the belief? I gave them a scenario. I walk into a pizzeria. The server is a White man. I, as you know, am a Black man. The White server BELIEVES that Black people are inferior to White people. He doesn't say this to me, nor does he act on it. He just believes it, thinks it, or it is one of the principles of his life. I ask him for a slice of pizza. He warms up my slice, gently gives it to me, I pay him and then go about my business, and he goes about his business.

I asked the class if the White man is racist. They said yes because of his beliefs. I then asked them to explain how his racism harmed me. They thought about it and concluded that it didn't. I asked, "How is racism harmful?" They again said that if he thinks Black people are inferior, then it's bad. I asked, "Who is allowed to determine what are good or bad thoughts?" And again, his thoughts didn't hurt me. If I think about committing murder but never do it, was it harmful? Will the cops arrest me if I think about murdering someone but never come close to acting on it? Did I break any laws? I asked the class if a man sees a beautiful woman and has "thoughts" (you get the point) about that woman, but never approaches her, did his "thoughts" hurt the woman? They said no. All men have "thoughts," but it is only a problem if they improperly act on them. Now ACTING on these thoughts is something different, isn't it?

If a person ACTS on their racist thoughts, is it still just racism? Or should the act be considered something else? I argued that racism could be harmless. If it is just a belief or a thought, who cares? We can't control people's thoughts. In most cases, we have no idea what people's beliefs are unless they tell us, or act on it. Again, is racism harmful? If another person only thinks or believes they are better than me, does it mean that they ARE better than me? If a person doesn't like me, should I let it dictate my actions if they never ACT on their belief? I debated with my students that racism could be harmless. I also pointed out that fighting racism or trying to end racism may be a losing battle. I asked them to come up with a plan to end racism. They said it was hard to do. One student felt it was a battle worth fighting, however, admitted they didn't know how to end it.

If racism is a belief, a train of thought, or a principle (not a rule), then isn't it harmless? Many Black Americans love fighting racism or trying to end racism. If you cannot fully control people's thoughts or beliefs, how is it possible to end racism? It's like ending hate. If you believe racism is hate toward another race, which is a common definition people give, then can you really end hate, which some believe is the root of racism? Hate has existed since the dawn of time. It will exist after we are all long gone from this Earth. You can't create laws to eliminate someone's beliefs. It is in their head. Isn't it a waste of energy on the part of Black Americans trying to end racism? If racism can be ended, then why hasn't Congress created a law outlawing racism? Wouldn't that end it and all our problems are solved as it relates to racism? Is there something ELSE Black Americans should focus their energy on fighting?

ARE YOU A RACIST?

I asked the students again if they were racist and if I was a racist. They said no. Understanding that hate or dislike isn't necessary for racism based on the definitions, they said they were not racist, and neither was I. I then told them that we are ALL racist. Their minds were open. They asked how. If I polled American adults and asked them if they were racist, most Americans would answer no. Then can someone please explain why America has racial issues if nobody is racist? When most people define racism, they do so in a manner that makes them personally not racist. Let's look at things from a different perspective. I challenged the class by asking how it is possible to believe there are different races and not be a racist. Analyze the definitions once again.

> *-a BELIEF that RACE is the primary determinant of human traits and capacities and that racial differences produce an INHERENT superiority of a particular race (Merriam-Webster)*

> *-racism is the BELIEF that people of some races are inferior to others, and the behavior which is the result of this belief (Oxford)*

-a BELIEF or doctrine that inherent differences among various human racial groups determine cultural or individual achievement, usually involving the idea that one's own race is superior and has the right to dominate others or that a particular racial group is inferior to the others (Dictionary.com)

-the BELIEF that humans may be divided into separate and exclusive biological entities called "races" (Britannica)

-policies, behaviors, rules that result in a continued unfair advantage to some people and unfair or harmful treatment of others based on race (Cambridge Dictionary)

If you believe there are different races, then do you not believe we look different due to a specific trait or traits? My students then pointed out that racism is also a belief in the superiority of a particular race over another. I said great, let's use that. I posed a question to my students, and I will pose the same question to you. You are at a basketball court. There is a team of 12 Black players and a team of 12 Asian players. You don't know anything else about the members of each team. The players all appear to be athletes. You must pick the winning team, and if you do, you will win $20 million. Which team would you pick? Only you would know the answer that you will give, but my students all universally said the Black players. I asked why.

They said that Black people are great at basketball, and Asians are not as much. I then asked them, "Wouldn't that mean you believe Blacks are SUPERIOR to Asians at basketball?" They paused. I pointed out that the definition did not specify superior in what way, just superior. Superiority could apply to anything a person chooses to apply it to. I asked them which team they thought most people would pick for $20 million. They said the Black players. I asked, "Then how is that not racist?" They believed that Black players were inherently better or superior at basketball than Asians. I asked, "You didn't know any members of each team, so why did you all universally pick the Black players?" They responded because Black people play basketball more than Asians (that's a belief). We don't even know if that is true. The Black players may have never played basketball; they could be hockey players. The Asians could be trained in basketball. I pointed out to the class that they made their pick based on the players' "race" and their belief that Black players are inherently superior to Asians at basketball, if not all sports, for that matter. Wouldn't that make you a racist? I pointed out to the class that they didn't know the culture of either side, so to say that Blacks play a lot of basketball is simply separating Blacks from other races (again, is this not racism?). Also, if most people would simply pick the Black team, couldn't that be unfair (not necessarily harmful) to the Asian players?

> *-the BELIEF that humans may be divided into separate and exclusive biological entities called RACES (Britannica)*

More simply if you believe that people are different due to race, then aren't you a racist? Clearly, if you believe that some people are Black or White, you BELIEVE that humans are divided into separate biological entities. Therefore, how can you believe in different races and not be racist? If you haven't noticed by now, the words racism or racist are derived from the word RACE. My students were thinking deeply. I never said or told them they were racist, but we were looking from a different perspective. Can we really end or fight racism? Is it possible we are fighting the wrong fight? Is it possible we, especially Black Americans, are confusing racism with a group of other words? If I BELIEVE I am 6'4" tall and handsome, does it change the fact that I am 5'8" and unattractive? Is a simple belief by itself inherently dangerous or harmful?

BIAS, PREJUDICE, DISCRIMINATION, OPPRESSION

I explained to the class that it is amazing how racism gets such a bad rap when you could argue it is harmless. One could argue it is the least offensive of other words that are associated with racism, which we will next examine. If I told you that you were racist, you would interpret that as me calling you Hitler. Was Hitler a racist? Yes. Did he believe that the so-called Aryan race was superior to the so-called Jewish race? Yes. Did he believe that Eastern Europeans were inferior? Yes. All true. However, Hitler had these beliefs in the 1920s when he had absolutely no power and nobody had ever heard of him. Not to mention that many other people not only in Germany but in Europe, held similar beliefs before the 1920s. Did his beliefs at the time harm any Europeans?

When he rose to power in the 1930s into the 1940s, he began ACTING on his beliefs. His beliefs in the 1920s were harmless, wouldn't you say? Or do you think his beliefs were still harmful? He didn't act on them. When he wrote *Mein Kampf* he was in prison. In fact, sales of the book didn't really skyrocket until he began taking power in Germany. Did he have the power to act on his beliefs? Could anyone in Europe have ended his beliefs, or his racism at the time? Not a chance. In fact, do we actually know what a person believes? Is it possible, however unlikely, that Hitler didn't even believe many of the things he said or put into print? I asked the class, is it possible, even if unlikely, that Hitler said things for political reasons and to scapegoat certain groups? Do politicians believe everything that comes out of their mouths? Do defense lawyers always believe their client is innocent while they are saying differently in court? The class acknowledged it was possible.

How can we know what a person truly believes? Do we know everything Hitler believed just because he put it in a book, or spoke it? I asked the students if they had ever said something contrary to what they believed and they all admitted they had. Could the same have applied to Hitler? They said that it could apply to Hitler; however, they all felt that he believed what he said and printed in his book. How can you control a person's beliefs? Is it possible? Some students said no, and one student with agreement from others, replied that you can to a certain extent if you can indoctrinate them, and even then, you still truly never know what a person believes. If racism is centered on belief, again I asked, how can we stop it? Is it worth trying to stop?

In the case of Hitler, one could argue the problems really began in the 1930s. Obviously, beliefs precede actions; however, if the belief never leads to action is it harmful? In fact, I pointed out to the students, *Mein Kampf* is still in print today. A recent CNN article entitled "How Hitler's *Mein Kampf* became a bestseller in 2016," discusses how public interest in the book is still strong today. I asked the students if beliefs by themselves are dangerous, shouldn't America and all countries ban books with dangerous beliefs? The students said that was not feasible. Also, as one student pointed out, who determines what is a dangerous belief? Couldn't it be argued that what Hitler did in the 1930s was not about belief, but was about action? Could it be that we are confusing words? Again, racism (a belief) can only do so much damage if it is simply in one's head. How can you end a living person's thoughts? What if the word racism or racist is being unfairly judged? I then asked the students to define four other words that are associated with racism. You do the same. The four words are BIAS, PREJUDICE, DISCRIMINATION, and OPPRESSION. Do not use a dictionary but define them as you understand them.

After the students wrote down their definitions, we looked up the words together.

BIAS

-bias implies an unreasoned and unfair distortion of judgment in favor of or against a person or thing (Merriam-Webster)

-the action of supporting or opposing a particular person in an unfair way (Cambridge)

-a particular tendency, trend, inclination, feeling, or opinion, especially one that is preconceived or unreasoned (Dictionary.com)

-a tendency to believe that some people, ideas, etc., are better than others that usually results in treating some people unfairly (Britannica.com)

-a PREFERENCE for one thing over another, especially an unfair one (Vocabulary.com)

-bias is a tendency to PREFER one person or thing over another, and to favor that person or thing (Collins English Dictionary)

After analyzing the term bias, I asked the class if it were possible that they'd confused racism with bias. They said yes. I asked them if racists are biased. They said, of course. I then asked them if they had any biases. They thought about it and acknowledged that they did. I pointed out that if they BELIEVED that Blacks are superior to Asians in basketball due to an inherent difference in race as they said earlier, could that make them racist based on the definition of racism? They were starting to see things from a different perspective. They could have challenged the notion, but they didn't. I said if racism is just a belief, do you still think it is dangerous as compared to bias? Does everyone have a bias? They said absolutely. Are biases harmful? They debated. They said they can be. They said it can be more harmful than racism because racism is just a belief, but when racism starts to influence our biases then biases are a little more dangerous, but not that much because a bias is still only an unreasonable opinion. They said bias and racism go hand in hand, and therefore the two were not that harmful if there was no action involved. I asked the class if it were possible to control a person's thoughts or feelings or opinions, and if so, how? One student commented that to a degree you can through indoctrination; however, if the individual is thinking freely without influence, then no, you cannot control a person's thoughts or feelings.

When a woman fills out a dating profile of the type of man she is looking for, she may say tall, dark, $100,000 income, no kids, etc. Is this biased? Or is it something else? Based on the definition of bias, the students believed that it was harmless bias. Her opinion is that is a better man or mate than someone who is short, not dark, makes $50,000 a year, and has two kids. Is this unreasonable? Maybe. Finding the type of man she wants may be highly unlikely. The point being everyone has a bias, according to the students. Can you end people's biases? The class said no, you can't. I argued, could it be possible to change a person's way of thinking to help change their biases? A student said that people individually must change their way of thinking, nobody can change another person's way of thinking. I asked how an individual can change their own way of thinking and the student replied, "By looking at things differently and trying to understand different points of view," which they said is hard to impossible for most people.

Next word, prejudice. On a sheet of paper, define the word prejudice without the use of a dictionary. The students wrote down their definitions, and I went around and asked them their responses. Most responses centered around treating people differently in an unfair manner. We then looked up definitions of the word.

PREJUCICE

-an unreasonable DISLIKE of or preference for a person, group, custom, etc., especially when it is based on their race, religion, sex, etc. (OxfordLearnersDictionaries.com)

-a bias or a preconceived opinion, idea, or belief about something (Dictionary. com)

-an unfair or unreasonable feeling especially when formed without enough thought or knowledge (Cambridge English Dictionary)

-an unfair feeling of DISLIKE for a person or a group because of their race, sex, religion, etc. (Britannica)

-an unreasonable DISLIKE of a particular group of people or things (Collins English Dictionary)

After looking at and analyzing the definitions of prejudice, the class made three observations. First, prejudice seemed very similar to bias. Next, they noticed that prejudice was rooted in feelings. Last, prejudice is mostly rooted in dislike, whereas bias could just be a preference for one thing over another, not necessarily a dislike. I asked the students, "Can you end prejudice?" They answered no. If it is a feeling of dislike, how can you legislate or control people's feelings? I asked them if racism is more dangerous than prejudice? They said racism involves prejudice, but I challenged that notion. I said prejudice is prejudice, and racism is racism. Why are we intermixing the words? I pointed out that these words are hard to define, which is why many times people intermix the words as the same. Maybe it is time to start looking at the words individually to simplify things. Remember, we are trying to look at things from a different perspective. They agreed that intermixing the words or comparing them as the same didn't make much sense. So far, the class consensus was that racism, bias, and prejudice can never be eradicated as they are rooted in belief, preference, and feelings of dislike.

We then looked at discrimination. I asked the students to write down their definition of discrimination on a sheet of paper, and I ask you the reader to do the same. Define discrimination. The students wrote down their definitions. Then, of course, we looked up the dictionary definition.

DISCRIMINATION

-TREATMENT or consideration of, or making a distinction in favor of or against a person or thing based on the group, class, or category to which that person belongs (Dictionary.com)

-the TREATMENT of a person or group of people differently, in a way that is worse than the way people are usually treated (Cambridge)

-the intended or accomplished differential TREATMENT of persons or social groups for reasons of certain generalized traits (Britannica)

-the practice of TREATING one person or group of people less fairly or less well than other people or groups (Collins Dictionary)

My students noticed something. There was one clear word that stood out in every definition. TREATMENT. In their definitions, they were mostly close to the actual dictionary definition of the word. They mentioned prevention or stopping a group of people, but all in all, they were able to recognize discrimination as an ACT. Keyword is TREATMENT. I asked the students if discrimination was harmful. They said absolutely. I asked them which is more harmful, racism (a belief or idea), or discrimination (treatment). They said clearly discrimination, as you can't control how a person thinks, as much as you may try, but you can control how a person ACTS to a certain degree. I asked them, can laws be created to control how people think or feel or what they believe? They said no. I asked, can laws be created to control how people act? They said absolutely. If I BELIEVE I am Superman, does that harm anyone by itself? If I believe I am Superman AND I try to fly off a building or run into a blazing fire acting on this belief, THEN is that dangerous? Are they different?

I asked, why do Black Americans (and other Americans) focus so much energy on ending racism? Why isn't more of that energy centered on ending discrimination? They really had no answer other than most people confuse the two words. When they say racism, could they really mean discrimination? I argued, then why don't we just say we need to end discrimination? They argued discrimination doesn't exist as much as it did in previous years. I asked, "Does racism still exist?" They said, sure it does. My point was that racism will never go away, but if discrimination is outlawed in America, why do Black people blame racism for problems in the Black community? Racism isn't an act; discrimination is. They started looking at things differently. Nobody wants to be labeled a racist because they think racism is the worst thing. If we are all racist because we buy into the concept of different races, then racism isn't the problem, or is it? Could acting on racism be the problem? (Which would be discrimination). They had never thought about it in that manner.

Again, if I order a slice of pizza and the White server thinks Black people are inferior to White people, but he serves me my pizza and I go about my business, did his racist belief hurt me in any way? They answered no. NOW if I order a slice of pizza and the White server charges me double the price because I am Black, does that hurt me? They said absolutely. I asked is that discrimination? They said yes because now it is an act. I asked, then why should I care what he believes? If he treats me fairly and equally, then that is all that matters. They agreed. Can we create laws to ensure that he does not discriminate and act on his racist beliefs? They said absolutely. I asked, would Black Americans be better off focusing on that than trying to control the minds of every single person and their beliefs? They said yes. They didn't have to agree. Just opening their minds to another perspective.

Many Black Americans will say they are held back by racism. One could argue it wasn't racism that held them back, it was discrimination. And in a nation where discrimination against Black Americans is not present today as it was 100 years ago, should Black Americans continue to use racism for any issues that they have if they can acknowledge racism isn't a major issue? Of course, that is only if they agree with that assessment. An earlier definition of racism I said I would refer to later was prejudice, discrimination, or antagonism directed against a person on the basis of membership in a particular racial group. If you must use the word prejudice and discrimination in the definition, couldn't one argue then it is not racism, it is just prejudice or discrimination? As far as antagonism, we will examine that in a bit. Lastly, I asked the students to define *oppression* on a sheet of paper. You, the reader, do the same. Do not use the dictionary.

OPRESSION

-unjust or cruel exercise of authority or power (Merriam-Webster)

-the exercise of authority or power in a cruel, burdensome, or unjust manner (Dictionary.com)

-a situation in which people are governed in an unfair and cruel way and prevented from having opportunities and freedom (Cambridge)

-to treat in a cruel or unfair way (Britannica)

Oppression also seemed easier for my students to define. They pretty much said that oppression was holding people down unfairly. When we analyzed the definitions of the word oppression, the class noticed a similar theme. Oppression involves people in power AND treatment that is unfair. Again, the word TREATMENT. Treatment is an act. Acts can be dangerous. Beliefs are not IF they stay a belief. I asked my students if they were oppressed. They said yes at first, but I asked them to explain how. I asked them to explain who their oppressors were. They couldn't and realized that their answer may have been preposterous. They went to school just like other groups, some had jobs, they had nice sneakers, cell phones, etc.

I asked them if slaves were oppressed. They said definitely. I then asked them if they are treated the same as slaves were back in the 1800s. Or were they treated the same as Black Americans in the 1950s and 1960s? They said no and realized that the "oppression" they believed they were living under today was not really oppression. Using the Hitler analogy, Hitler was a racist because he believed Jews were inferior, but could it be that his racism was harmless to German Jews in the 1920s? Hitler was biased, as he was not in favor of Jews. Was his bias a threat? Hitler was prejudiced, as he clearly didn't like Jews. Again, it was a feeling. Was his prejudice a threat by itself? When he rose to power in Germany is the point at which he had the power to act. If he had never acted on those feelings, would it have been harmful to Jewish people? If he believed Jews were inferior, favored other Germans over Jews, and had a dislike of Jews, however ensured that Germany's laws protected all citizens INCLUDING Jews, would racism, bias, or prejudice really have been a problem for Jewish people? Some students still believed that racism, bias, and prejudice was a problem for a country's leader. How much of a problem, however, they did not know. Other students believed that if laws were equally enforced, who cared what the leader thought? You can't control it anyway, and what leader in history didn't have a bias or prejudice?

When Hitler began to discriminate against and oppress Jewish people, was that the real issue? Is trying to stop a person's feelings worth the energy, or is ensuring that discrimination and or oppression never happens a better use of that energy? How many owners in Major League Baseball signed Black players after Jackie Robinson entered the league? More and more owners signed Black players and paid them tremendous amounts of money. Many Black players in American sports have gained tremendous wealth playing for racist owners. The most prominent modern-day example is Donald Sterling, former owner of the Los Angeles Clippers. He was racist, biased, and prejudiced. However, how many Black players played on his team over the years, making millions of dollars and building generational wealth? Did he specifically discriminate against Black players and only attempt to field White players, which he could have tried to do, although it wouldn't have looked good? Sure. He didn't discriminate because, in the end, he wanted to compete with the other teams. Black players who played for the Clippers did well. His racist, biased, and prejudiced opinions did not harm them. Had he begun to discriminate or oppress, that would have been different.

The students were very open-minded. Should people worry about racism and ending it, or just focus on discrimination and oppression? Should slogans say, "End Racism" or should they say, "End Oppression?" If the word oppression doesn't seem viable to use as a slogan because oppression doesn't really exist in America as it did previously, could it then mean that Black Americans have made tremendous progress and no longer must worry about racism "holding them back?" If my students have never faced oppression or discrimination, could it be possible they are not successful due to their OWN decisions and actions? Should more Black Americans have this attitude?

This does not mean that discrimination or oppression does not exist in America still to this day. It does. How much discrimination or oppression is there? Has discrimination and oppression diminished in the last 100 years? Fifty years? Twenty-five years? Even though there is plenty of work to be done, have Black Americans made tremendous strides in tearing down racial discrimination and oppression? No right or wrong answers, just a DIFFERENT PERSPECTIVE. As a class, after analyzing the different words and terms, we decided to simplify everything and reanalyze things. Below are the simplified definitions the students came up with:

RACISM- *BELIEF/IDEA people are DIFFERENT due to race; if you believe there are different races, you believe there are differences in people; if there are differences, then everything can't be equal among people, meaning some are superior to others in different situations.*

BIAS- *Having a PREFERENCE toward something, someone, a group, or having a FAVOR for something over another*

PREJUDICE- *DISLIKING something, or a feeling of dislike of something or a group of people.*

DISCRIMINATION- *TREATING people or groups differently*

OPPRESSION- *Cruel use of POWER*

Next, we analyzed each word, and the class, based on consensus, had to rank the words in order of danger to Black Americans, 1 being the most dangerous, 5 being the least. Here was the class consensus:

RACISM-5

BIAS- 4

PREJUDICE- 3

DISCRIMINATION- 2

OPPRESSION- 1

The class believed that racism was the least worrisome of the words, and discrimination and oppression were by far the worst. How would you rank them? On a sheet of paper, rank the words based on how dangerous you believe them to be to society. There are no right or wrong answers. How do your rankings compare?

PRESIDENTIAL RACISM

Another big discussion among Black Americans is whether presidents are racist. Earlier in the discussion on racism, I asked the students if it matters if a president is racist. There was a presidential election in the U.S. the year before I first taught this course. I asked the students who they would have voted for in the election if they were able to vote. They picked the Democrat over the Republican. I asked why. The first and most common answer was that the Republican candidate was racist. I asked how, and one student went through a list of things that he perceived as racist. I responded OK, so you believe him to be racist. I asked him do you believe the Democrat to be a racist? He said no.

After doing some research, I brought in some evidence to the class that suggested that the Democrat the above student would have voted for also had said or done some questionable things that could be considered racist. The student then said that the Republican candidate was more racist. I pointed out two things to challenge the student. I asked how do you determine who is more racist? Also, if you consider both to be racist, then should it matter? I also argued if both are racist, is it harmful if they enforce the law fairly? The student said it should matter. The student readily admitted that they were biased. I appreciated the honesty. The same student even created a presentation detailing that the Republican candidate was a terrible racist and presented it to the class. However, I challenged the student's presentation. In front of the class, he acted as a prosecutor pressing charges against the Republican candidate, while I acted as the defense attorney. The class understood that this did not indicate whether or not I voted for the Republican candidate, as they had no idea who I voted for. I hope you as the reader understand that as well.

Many Black Americans will say they will vote for one candidate over another because of racism when one could argue both are racist. All the students in the class said that they would vote for the Democratic candidate because they viewed the Republican candidate as a racist. I asked, shouldn't policy be more important? Whatever a person finds most important in a candidate when choosing to vote is up to that person and they can never be wrong in their choice. For some, it can be about the candidate's immigration policy or their religious beliefs.

Black Americans can exhibit extreme bias when picking a candidate to vote for, as all Americans are prone to do. I wanted to point out a different perspective to the students. The Democratic candidate for president that the student supported over the Republican candidate in an interview stated that any Black American who did not vote for him wasn't really Black. Or as he put it, "You ain't Black." I asked the student if that was a racist comment. Who is he (a White man) to tell a Black person they are not Black unless they vote for him? The student acknowledged it was a racist comment but stuck to his guns that the Republican candidate was "more racist."

The rest of the class had a different take. At first, they were all in agreement that the Republican candidate was a blatant racist, and that Black Americans should not vote for him. When I pointed out that the Democratic candidate had some questionable racist quotes, and provided evidence of it, most of the class began to change their tune. They argued that if they can consider both to be racist (and I never told them the candidates were or were not racist, I am playing devil's advocate to their beliefs), then does racism really matter? Shouldn't your choice of who you vote for be based on policy rather than racism if they are both racist in your eyes? Or do you go with the candidate you view as less racist? The rest of the class started to challenge their own assessments. However, one student was adamant that the Republican candidate was not good because he was racist and had a past of discriminatory behavior. It was a great debate between the lone student and other members of the class.

I pointed out that when I asked which candidate you would vote for and your answer was the Democratic candidate because the Republican candidate was racist, then I assumed racism was the most important issue since it was the first thing you mentioned. Many (not all) Black Americans will say they will not vote for a candidate because he or she is "racist." If we understand that we are all possibly racist, then can you still use that assessment? The rest of the class started to look at things in a different way. Some of the students did not know of the questionable racist statements made by the Democratic candidate they were so eager to support over the Republican candidate.

Gaining knowledge of the facts that were presented to them, they started asking more about their policies. The one student, however, reaffirmed their belief that the Republican candidate was more racist, and they were supporting the lesser of two evils. The student also recognized their bias. Again, no right or wrong answers. Just different perspectives. Does it matter if a president is racist? Couldn't it be argued that every president in American history was a racist to some degree, if only by default that they believed in the concept of race, which would mean they had to have believed in an inherent difference between people? If a president is racist, does that mean that Black Americans cannot live and function well in society? If a president is racist, but enforces the laws equally and does not discriminate or oppress, does his racist beliefs matter, or have any impact on Black Americans positively or negatively?

I asked the class if they believed Abraham Lincoln was a racist. They said absolutely, there is no way he believed that Whites and Blacks were equal. I then pointed out that he was instrumental in freeing the slaves and "ending" slavery(as a class we had a deep discussion on if slavery really came to an end). In fact, Carter G. Woodson, the founder of "Negro History Week", the precursor to Black History Month, in 1926 picked the second week of February to celebrate Negro History Week. Why? To honor the birthdays of Frederick Douglass AND Abraham Lincoln on the 12th and 14th of February. Even though Abraham Lincoln may have been a racist in the eyes of the class, did his racism harm Black slaves when he played a part in their freedom? Did the White abolitionists during those times believe Blacks and Whites were different? Probably. Could that make them racist? Maybe. They still wanted to end slavery. If they were possibly racist also, how did their racism hurt Black slaves? Is racism the real enemy?

If all politicians and government officials are racist, but they do not discriminate or oppress and they equally create, enforce and judge the laws of the land, does racism harm Black Americans or any Americans? Many times, I've heard people as diverse as Nancy Reagan and Denzel Washington ask, "Which is more important, what happens in the White House or your own house?" The students now had a different perspective on this matter than when we started the discussion. Again, it doesn't mean they had to agree. It was a different perspective.

SYSTEMIC RACISM, SYSTEMIC DISCRIMINATION, OR SYSTEMIC OPPRESSION?

My students agreed that racism and oppression were totally different things, and they agreed that oppression was far worse. I asked the class to define systematic racism. How would you define it? We looked up definitions and found many of them. We analyzed a couple and came up with the definition below.

Systemic Racism

-policies and practices that exist throughout a whole society or organization, and that result in and support a continued unfair advantage to some people and unfair or harmful treatment of others based on race (Cambridge)

Next, we looked up systemic discrimination. Again, many different definitions. Can you define it? Many definitions did not come from an actual dictionary; however, we picked one from the Google search we did.

Systemic Discrimination

-practices or attitudes that have, whether by design or impact, the effect of limiting an individual's or a group's right to opportunities generally available (Manitoba Canada Human Rights)

Next, we looked up systemic oppression. Can you define it? Once again, many definitions, but not many from an actual dictionary. We decided to use the following definition:

Systemic Oppression

-the intentional disadvantaging of groups of people based on their identity while advantaging members of the dominant group (gender, race, class, sexual orientation, etc.) (National Equity Project)

The class analyzed the three terms and came up with the consensus that the three terms sounded extremely similar. We looked at systematic racism and noticed that it mentioned practices in the definition.

Again, practice is an act, which would move it beyond a belief into action, which the class acknowledged earlier was more dangerous than a belief. The class looked at the definitions and agreed that systemic racism was again being entangled with the words systemic discrimination and systemic oppression.

I asked my students if they were victims of systemic discrimination or systemic oppression. You the reader, no matter what race you are, answer this question. Some of my students believed they faced oppression, but once they saw the definition, they changed their answers. They said they never experienced oppression. I asked the students, have Black Americans been the victims of systemic discrimination and/or oppression at any point in American history? They responded absolutely. Undeniable fact. I asked, "Are Black Americans the victims of systemic discrimination?" They weren't sure. What about systemic oppression?

Some of the students brought up incidents like the police murder of George Floyd, which at the time of this writing was two years prior so it was still fresh in people's minds. I asked the students if the murder of George Floyd was a product of a SYSTEM that murdered him, or a police officer individually murdering him? I asked if the SYSTEM was responsible for the murder of George Floyd, why did the police who murdered him get convicted of a crime? When slaves were beaten or tortured by their masters, did the system punish them? They said no. I asked if systemic oppression exists today in the way it existed in the 1800s in America? They said no, but it may still exist. They said that today as in the mid-1950s police disproportionately targeted Black Americans, and they also pointed out issues like Hurricane Katrina in Black neighborhoods being ignored. However, is there a systemic policy to specifically target Black Americans? Also, could the disproportionate targeting by police be due to SOME behaviors by Black Americans, especially young Black Americans? I also asked if there were laws that specifically discriminated against Black Americans or specifically oppressed Black Americans.

They acknowledged there were no laws, but in many circles of government it was "unwritten." In the course we do a unit on Police and The Black Experience, but that will not be covered in this book. I asked the students if they believed they would not succeed or could not succeed due to their "race" in America. They said systemic oppression or discrimination will not prevent them from being successful. The consensus of the class was there may be discrimination, and most certainly racism, but they were unsure if it was a systemic problem. In the past, they brought up evidence of clear systemic oppression, such as the FBI and its illegal activities during the 1960s against Black civil rights groups. Examples such as the FBI's illegal monitoring of the Black Panther Party or wiretapping of Martin Luther King Jr. What about the present day? Again, no right or wrong answers. Sometimes the best answer is "I don't know," as it may encourage a person to seek out answers. What do you think?

IS AMERICA RACIST?

When I ask this question, people of different races interpret it very differently. If you ask some White Americans this question, they may get extremely emotional and defensive. First, and foremost, they think I am making a statement. Second, they interpret the question as, "Are you racist?" Third, they hear the question and believe I am asking are White people racist, almost as if America is synonymous with White people. If you ask some Black Americans the same exact question, they will interpret it as me asking, are White Americans racist? And the overwhelming response is yes, Americans (but in their minds White people) are all racist. What some Black Americans fail to realize is that the question includes ALL Americans, including Black Americans. Are there racist Black Americans? We all know the answer to that, just as there are racist Asian Americans, Hispanic Americans, and so on and so forth. There have been arguments that Black Americans are just as racist as all other groups in America, if not more racist, so why do Black Americans focus so much on racism in America without pointing the blame first at Black Americans? I showed the class an article written for usnews.com by Steven Nelson in 2013 titled "Poll Finds Black Americans More Likely To Be Seen As Racist." The article found that 37% of poll respondents believed most Black Americans are racist. Fifteen percent of respondents believed most Whites are racist, and 18% believed most Hispanics are racist. When the question is asked about America being a racist nation, how are people interpreting the question? Americans are so indoctrinated into division, that a question that encompasses ALL Americans can easily be fragmented and interpreted differently.

If we can acknowledge that all races of people in America can be racist, would that make America racist? Maybe, or maybe not. If most Americans simply believe in the idea of different races, and that people of these various races are inherently different, could this be racism? The question was not does America discriminate or oppress, it is simply, is America racist? One question that was asked was, "Based on what criteria?" I purposely did not give criteria as I wanted the students to go with their natural inclination, and I would ask you, the reader, to do the same. Some people will look at the question and encompass the entire history of America from its very beginning to today. Others will look at the question and only base their answer on the present day. Some will pick and choose different time periods and use that to represent America. No right or wrong answers, just a question. My students gave various answers to the question.

I asked, "If you believe that America is a racist nation, is that a bad thing?" I asked them to name a nation in history that was never racist. Can you? If every nation on Earth may have been or is racist, why would America be any different? And again, does racism by itself stop people from being successful? A common misconception in America is that White Americans are the only racist people. My Black students pointed out that they knew several racist Black people in their lives. My Hispanic students pointed out they knew several racist Hispanics. Also, can you be racist against your own race? The students said absolutely. They said a Black person can believe that Blacks are inferior to Whites intellectually, for example. Why do people assume that if a person is Black, they can't be racist against other Blacks? Why doesn't that count as racism?

If a Black person sees a White person who can dance well, would many Black people be shocked? If a Black person said to a White person who can dance that they dance well for a White person, is that not antagonistic (it could be seen as hostile or insulting)? My students responded yes. I asked why. Are White Americans inherently inferior dancers to Black Americans? My students jokingly said yes, it's rare.

If you believe that to be true, and you're judging a person's ability to dance based on their race, isn't that racist? If a person of any race walks into an Asian restaurant and asks to meet the owner and I, a Black man, walk out, would that shock people? The students said absolutely. I asked why. They responded that it isn't normal because I am Black. I asked, isn't that a belief that I cannot own or operate an Asian restaurant? They responded that it is not Black culture. I then said culture and race are different things. Culture is a way of life. How could you possibly know what culture I was raised in? You're just assuming based on my "race." What if I was raised in an Asian household, and spoke fluent Chinese? If you judge a person's actions based on their race, how is that not racism? You don't know my culture until you get to know me personally. Speaking of culture.

I asked the students if a young White woman visits her parents and brings a young Black man to her house and says that he is her boyfriend and she wants to marry him, do you think most White parents would be OK with it? They said no. Some would, most would not. If a young Black man brings home a young White girl in the same scenario, do you think most Black parents would be OK with it? The Black girls said in most cases no, especially the mother of the young Black boy. If an American girl whose family is of Indian descent and practices Hinduism brings home a young Mexican American boy, do you think her parents would approve? The class said most would not. Some sure, but not most. I asked why, and what would be the problem?

I said the first response of the parents is the honest response. If they would initially have problems in all three scenarios, isn't that racism? The students said they may want their child to marry someone of their culture. I pointed out how could you possibly know the culture of the boyfriend or girlfriend; you just met them. The parents initially are clearly judging the young man or woman they are being introduced to based on their race. I asked the students if they believed this would be normal in America, would that make America a racist nation? Even though (according to them) the parents may not want their child dating someone of a different race, did that necessarily mean they HATED members of that race? As mentioned earlier, according to most definitions, HATE is not necessary to be considered racism or racist.

I introduced another viewpoint. Many people point to the election of Barack Obama in 2008, and his reelection in 2012 as a sign that America is not a racist nation. How or why would a nation elect a "Black" man president if it were a racist nation? Undoubtedly Black, as well as many White, Hispanic, and Asian Americans voted for him. In the wake of the murder of George Floyd, Black as well as White, Hispanic, AND Asian Americans protested in the streets together against police brutality. I showed the students images of White Americans wearing Black Lives Matter shirts, and even organizing Black Lives Matter rallies. If America were racist, would this happen? (There is a unit on Black Lives Matter in the course.) In the fight for civil rights of the 1950s and 1960s, many White Americans worked with Black civil rights leaders to end racial discrimination and oppression. Many non-Blacks have fought alongside Black Americans to bring racial equality. Also, many people of many different races immigrate to America willingly. Would they do this if America was such a racist nation? Can we call America a racist nation? Again, it depends on interpretation, or a person's perspective or experiences.

WHAT IF WE ARE ALL RACIST?

The reason racism is hard to discuss is that race itself is hard to discuss. If race is hard to define, then racism is even harder to define. Both are rooted in beliefs. The idea of race has changed a few times over the course of history. I asked the class, "Who came up with these ideas?" Were they challenged? How long has the idea existed? What is the point of having different races? Some people will argue that racism doesn't exist like it did hundreds of years ago. There is no doubt today that open racism is much more frowned upon than it was 100 years ago. How can we accurately measure if there is less racism today than there was 100 years ago? Just because racism isn't in public and in your face doesn't mean there is less of it today as opposed to 100 years ago. How do we know what a person is saying in their home when nobody is around? How would I ever know if a White person I know, who smiles to my face and is friendly to me in public, isn't calling me the N-Word, or insulting me because of my race, in their home? Unless there is a recording of it, I would never know. Speaking of which, how many non-black entertainers have we seen who work with Black

Americans, and get caught using racial slurs when they think nobody is listening or they are drunk or angry and emotional? (This is more prejudice and discrimination than racism.) Then the entertainer issues a public apology that they are "not a racist?" How can we measure the nation's racism accurately? The class agreed, it is impossible.

The class wanted to look at it from a different perspective. Racism is the start of it all. Racism is the umbrella that racial bias, prejudice, discrimination, and oppression fall under. Racism is the root. However, if the root never grows, do you ever get a tree? What if we are all racist, AND we acknowledge it? What if we acknowledge that by buying into the belief or idea of different "races," that inherently makes us ALL racist, Black, White, Asian, and so on and so forth? Now, can I ever point to another person and condemn them for being a racist, if I am a racist as well? What if the words racism and racist aren't as bad as they have been made out to be? If we can all acknowledge that we are racist, now perhaps we can move to the next word on the list. Bias. Are we all biased? One could argue everyone is biased, but not everyone is biased about race. Now I may be a racist just like you, but you may be biased against different races, while I may not be. You and I may both be racist, but I may not have a dislike for other races as you may (prejudice). We all may be racists, but you may treat other races differently and unfairly whereas I refuse to do so (discrimination). And again, we may all be racist, but I refuse to oppress those based on their race while you may have no problem in doing so (oppression).

Would this help us focus our energy on what really matters? Does this also help us to identify our flaws better, and ensure that though we are all racist, we should work on the other words that gradually get worse? This way we can stop focusing on the word that is the least dangerous (at least according to my students). Is it hard to prove if a person is racist or not if it is all in the head? Can you easily prove if someone is biased, prejudiced, discriminatory, or oppressive based on their ACTIONS? Should we all just acknowledge we are all racists?

If you constantly search for racism, chances are you will find it one could argue. Do we focus on not being racist so much that we ignore the other words that are associated with it? Do we focus on not being racist so much that when we feel we aren't racist we stop, and are content and we do not work on not being biased or prejudiced? Or since racism is the root of it all, should we focus on racism more to cut out the root so that it can never form a tree? Most of the class was more concerned with the other words than with racism; however, one student still believed that it was important to try and end racism even if it was nearly impossible to do. I gave the students an analogy to consider. Black Americans generally want to end racism. What if we view racism like death, and oppression and discrimination like murder? Can our society stop death? The obvious answer from the class was no. We are all going to die, so why spend so much energy trying to eliminate death? Not to say that we shouldn't try to help people live and stave off the process of dying, but in the end, we will all die. Society however, can do a lot to limit and/or reduce murder through laws and severe consequences. Couldn't this be the same for oppression and discrimination? We may never completely eradicate our society of oppression and discrimination just like murder, however, we can have a major impact on stopping it. Racism, like death, is a part of life. Oppression and discrimination, like murder, don't have to be. Shouldn't more of our energy go towards that? What do you think? No right or wrong answers. Just a different perspective.

Questions To Consider/Answer

Do you view racism as dangerous to society? If so, how would you end racism in America? Or do you view racism as not that big a deal and overblown in comparison to other words? And if you believe this, why?

Would you consider yourself a racist? Why or why not?

Does it matter if a president, a police officer, or a government official is a racist if they treat all Americans equally in the eyes of the law?

Do you believe Americans can check their biases if they can acknowledge them?

Do you believe America is a racist nation? Why or why Not?

CHAPTER SIX

THE "N-WORD"

AN UGLY WORD

The N-word. Another word or term or topic that, if left out of a discussion about Black Americans and their experiences simply put, would be an inauthentic discussion. As stated earlier, this course discusses things that are not normally discussed in a public high school. When I introduced the topic to my students, I explained that I've heard many people say that nigger is the ugliest, most horrific word in the English language. They agreed. Again, I think most people who aren't biased, prejudiced, or discriminatory toward Black/African Americans would agree it is an ugly, disgusting word. If you wanted to quiet a room full of people speaking, and you yelled the word at the top of your lungs, it would completely silence the room. Immediately people would become insulted, and many people would be offended (and not just Black/African Americans). The word is so disgusting that most people just refer to it as the "N-Word." In fact, for some, seeing the word in print will be hard.

Where did this word come from? If the word is so disgusting, why don't Americans just agree never to use or refer to it? Why don't we as Americans just destroy the word forever? One reason is that some people clearly want to use the word as an insult. If a person who is not Black, but White, for example, uses the word toward a Black person, they are automatically labeled a racist (which is why the word racist gets such a bad connotation). One could argue however, from a different perspective that is not racism, that it is prejudice (dislike) or discrimination (treating a person of a group differently) because they would not use the slur as an insult toward a White person in most cases. In cases involving members of the government (such as instances of police abuse of Black Americans where the word has been used), it can be considered a form of oppression.

Before we continue, we will look up definitions of the word "nigger" using different dictionary definitions.

Nigger

-an extremely offensive word for a Black person (Collins English Dictionary)

-used as an insult and contemptuous term for any dark-skinned person (Merriam-Webster)

My students as well as you, the reader, know what the word stands for. We really don't need to look up more definitions, although you may feel free to do so. Nigger was first used as a synonym for negro. The word nigger was never intended to be used to define someone as "ignorant" or "stupid," as many people believe it to be. For many years there has been a longstanding joke of Black people vs. niggers in the Black community, and how niggers ruin things for Black people. Today in some cases, Black Americans will use it in reference to other Black Americans. Have you ever heard the N-Word used in person? Do you know anyone who uses the N-Word? Do YOU use the N-Word?

NIGGER VS. NIGGA

When walking through the halls of the high school where I work, you will see the hallways filled with students in between classes. Some on their way to class, some talking, some making out, some hanging out, and so on and so forth. Ask any teacher in my building, or any teacher in an average public school like mine and they will know exactly what I am talking about. Students are yelling, talking loudly, and of course, using language that you wouldn't find in a church. There is one word that is extremely popular among many students in my high school, and again I'm sure in many high schools across the nation. The word "NIGGA." Not NIGGER. My class had a deep discussion. For some of you, you may not see the difference between the words NIGGER and NIGGA. Clearly, they are spelled differently. To you the reader, they may mean the same thing. Too many of our youth (this is not exclusive to Black students), they mean totally different things.

Nigger is a clear insult. We know that. What about the word nigga? I pointed out to the students the same observation I made earlier about students in the hallways. The same goes on in classrooms as well. The students acknowledged the use of the word nigga is prevalent in our high school. I asked them why students use such a hateful word. (I know how they are using it isn't in a hateful manner, but I was leading up to a different perspective.) The students explained that the word "nigga" was not an insult. In fact, the students explained that the word was a "term of endearment." I laughed. "A term of endearment," I asked? They said yes. The class explained that the word nigger was an insult, but that nigga was a greeting, and a show of respect and love for a friend. I asked them if the word nigger was a good word to use and they said no.

I asked them why would you use a word (nigga) as a term of love that is in such a close relationship to a word (nigger) that is a term of hate? Again, they told me it was a "term of endearment." One student explained it was like calling your friend "brother." I politely responded, "Then instead of calling your friend nigga, why not call him brother?" In fact, just like you dropped the "er" off the word nigger to make it endearing and sound cool, you can drop the "er" from brother and call him your "brotha" to make it sound cool. Among the youth in America, any word that ends in "er" instantly becomes cool if you replace the "er" with an "a", such as gangster to "gangsta." They said it didn't work that way. I asked why not. They couldn't give me any real answer.

I asked the students if they used the word nigger. They all said no. I asked if they used the word nigga. All but one Hispanic student in the class said they did. When I asked the Hispanic student why they didn't use it, they explained that they felt it was wrong and shouldn't be used, especially by someone who was not Black. The other students insisted it was not an insult and was OK to use. Again, they reiterated that it was a "term of endearment." I then restated that the word nigga was a term of endearment. They said absolutely. I said OK, no problem. I told one student the next time he saw his grandmother, walk up to her, kiss her on the cheek and say, "What's up my nigga?", the same way the students in our school use the vernacular. The students laughed, and the one student said, "No way." I asked, "Why not?" The student said it would be highly inappropriate.

I asked since they said it was a term of endearment, why wouldn't they use it towards their grandmother? The student explained nigga was in line with a curse word. I asked if it is an inappropriate word to use, and is equal to a curse word, how is it a term of endearment, AND why would you use it in a school setting. I see many of my White colleagues who become very uncomfortable when they hear the multitude of students in my school using the word. Many (most) I am sure are afraid to say anything to the students. First, the students wouldn't listen anyway, and second because of the racial component that I am sure none of them want to touch. I get it. Not to say that some of my White colleagues won't say anything.

I explained to the students that I hear it so often, I must just ignore it because there isn't enough time in the day or breath in my lungs to try to get students to stop using it. However, a student pointed out to me that, as a Black educator, I did have a responsibility to call it out when I hear it. They are right. I do and I have. However there are times I must get to class, and I don't have the leisure to stop every time I hear the word in passing in the hall to lecture students about using the word. My student however was not wrong. At all. I challenged my students not to use the word for one weekend. They agreed they would try. The following Monday, I asked them how they did. The Black students said they used it, but far less now that they were aware that they were using it so nonchalantly. They still believed it was OK to use. One Hispanic student never used the word, and the Native American student didn't give a response either way. I asked the class if they thought I used the word nigga. The class was split. Some said yes, and some said no. And of course, I didn't tell them whether I did or didn't.

"IT'S OUR WORD NOW"

I asked the students in the class why they felt it necessary to continue using the word nigga. A couple of students said that over time they have changed the meaning of the word. Nigger is a harmful word, but nigga is positive. One student said that the word now belonged to Black people and that Black Americans have changed the narrative surrounding the word. I asked why would you want to keep such a hateful word alive in the English language. They responded that there was a clear difference between the words nigger and nigga. Nigga, as they continued to point out to me, was a positive word. I asked them, if Martin Luther King Jr., Malcolm X, Frederick Douglass, or Booker T. Washington heard Black Americans using the word nigga, would they be happy? Is that what they were hoping for when they fought for the rights and better treatment of Black/African Americans? They said no. However, times change. Some students acknowledged that it isn't proper to use the word, especially in a public setting. They also acknowledged that the word is so ingrained or indoctrinated into their vocabulary that it is almost impossible to stop using it. It would take time, possibly years, to undo the use of the word, if they wanted to stop using the word. I never told them to stop using the word. They are big boys and girls. I don't tell the students what to think, or what to do. My job is just to show a different perspective. If young Black Americans (and older Black Americans, to a degree) believe that the word belongs to Black Americans, then it will be almost impossible for Black Americans to stop using the word. If Black Americans view the word as completely different than the word nigger, even though that is the root of the word, they will continue to use the word. In continuing to use the word nigga, the class did agree that it keeps the word nigger alive and popular. Some students acknowledged it is up to individual not to use the word nigger. Again, they believed it belonged to Black Americans. Great. I pointed out a problem with their theory. If it belongs to Black Americans, why do we hear other races or groups use the word constantly as well?

WHO CAN USE THE WORD NIGGA?

I showed the class a video of a White teacher in Alabama who was suspended from his school and reprimanded for calling a Black student nigga. When interviewed on the local news, the teacher replied that he used the word nigga, not nigger. He repeated both words in the interview. He explained that he hears Black students use it all the time and that the student used the word toward him first, and he simply was using it back toward the student. He believed the word not to be a big deal because of its constant usage by students in the school. The students were dumbfounded at how he could use the word. I asked them if he should be suspended. They said yes, absolutely. He can't use that word. I asked the class if I used the word toward a student, what would the response be? They said most students would think it was cool. I asked what's the difference between me and the teacher in the video? They said that I was cool (in reality, they were saying that I am Black) and it is OK for me to use it even though they acknowledged that as a teacher it is inappropriate.

I asked would most students care that it was inappropriate. They responded no. I then asked if I should be suspended or reprimanded. They struggled with the answer because they knew where I was going. I pointed out that was hypocritical. One student responded yes, but it is different. It is OK if I as a Black person used the word, but it is not OK for a White man to use the word. They did see the hypocrisy. I asked the class if Black students in our high school were the only group to use the word nigga. The class said no, and they were 100 percent correct. Teaching in this school for 19 years, I have heard all different types of people using the word. My district and school, for that matter, has always had a mix of Black, White, and Hispanic students. The population mix within those groups has changed over the years, but it is still what most would call a diverse school. In my high school, Black students are not the only ones using the word nigga on a regular basis. Students who are White and Hispanic use the word as well.

When I pointed this out in class, I told the class that I was confused. I thought that word belonged to "Black" people. In fact, I've seen many non-Blacks use the term in speaking to Black students. Not as an insult, but as a term of endearment as the students pointed out. If the word belongs to "Black" people, shouldn't every Black student tell the non-Black students not to use the word? They explained it was part of the culture of young people today (it was the same back when I was in high school as well). Why should a White teacher who uses the word get suspended for using it, but a Black teacher (myself) who uses it shouldn't get in trouble or a non-Black student who uses it should not get in trouble also? I pointed out that the rules on who can use it were not only hypocritical but extremely biased.

One student stated that they believed nobody but Black people should use the word. They reiterated that Black people owned the word now. I pointed out to them that the word nigger came from White people, so how do Black people own the word nigga, since it originated with White people? Technically shouldn't they be the ones to use the word since they created it and "own" it? The class was dumbfounded. They didn't know how to respond. I pointed out that many Black Americans get angry when White people start doing things that culturally belong to Blacks. If nigger came from White people, shouldn't they get angry at Black people for changing and using the word? The class couldn't argue back.

I also asked how did Black Americans come to "own" the word? Did Black Americans trademark the word legally and now it belongs to the "Black community?" Also, who is to say who is White or Black? I thought that we had the freedom to pick our race in this country. What if that "White" teacher identified as a "Black" man? Was his skin not dark enough? Are light-skinned Black people allowed to use the word nigga? Is their skin dark enough? I was opening pandora's box. One student said they would not be bothered if a White person said the word nigga in addressing them. As the student pointed out again, it is a term of endearment. They would be totally fine with it. I said OK, that is great, at least you are not being a hypocrite. I then said to the student that since they were OK with a White person using the term toward them in conversation, then they should or would have no issue with a bald White man with swastika tattoos holding a Confederate flag using the word nigga in his direction. The students' lips started to form a smile and it was obvious they were in deep thought.

The student responded that they would not be OK with that. I asked why not. They clearly said they were OK with a White man using the word, AND the word nigga is a term of endearment. The White man with swastikas and the Confederate flag fits both criteria, so it shouldn't be a problem if he uses the word nigga. The student said it was different; he was a racist. I asked the student how are you judging who is a racist and who is not when they use the term nigga? The student had a hard time answering. I also asked who makes up the rules on who can use the word. As seen in the class, one person's opinion or perspective can be vastly different than someone else's. It does get very confusing. If a student from Norway came to America and heard the use of the word as often as it is used here and used it toward a Black student, they may get offended and try to fight the student from Norway. In that student's defense, they may have heard it so often that they thought it was part of the English vernacular. Can you blame them? How would they have known not to use the word? What rule book was given to them?

I asked the students if it was OK for Black people to use the word nigga toward other Black people? They said yes, that was perfectly fine and acceptable. I then pointed out that Black people are not all one formative group. What if a Black person uses the word nigga to another Black person and that Black person finds the word offensive? One student replied that it is not offensive (once again a greeting, or a "term of endearment"). I pointed out to that student that you cannot tell a person how they should feel about a word that is used toward them, ESPECIALLY a word that is derived from the word nigger. I also said to the students that one could argue it is a complete myth that the word nigga is a term of endearment. They asked how. I pointed out that I have seen several disagreements and verbal altercations in my 19+ years in the high school. Many times, when students are in an altercation, they are using the word nigga toward their opponent. They acknowledged it as well. I asked the class if the word is a term of endearment, why do we constantly hear students yelling out the word nigga in a hostile situation if it means "brother" or friend? They could see where I was going with it. They really had no concrete answer. It does not mean they will stop using the word, but they did acknowledge that I had a point. They were seeing a different perspective.

The whole notion of who can use and who cannot use the word nigga was very confusing. The class agreed that nigger should NEVER be used. Absolutely, no way. I asked them, OK, what about historical films about slavery? Again, they had to pause. There are many films based on slavery that use the word nigger. Is that OK? They said that since it is a historical film, it was OK for the word to be used in a historical context for the film. I challenged them that they just said the word nigger should NEVER be used, and already they had made an exception. I pointed out how this could be confusing. They acknowledged it. If a racist actor said the word nigger in a historical slavery film, then it shouldn't bother them. They said no, it would. Even more confusing.

Back to nigga. Rappers use the word constantly. I assume they believe that the word belongs to the Black community as well. There have been non-Black singers and rappers who have used the word and been criticized for it. I argued with the class that some people didn't see the big deal. If they are doing "Black" music, then they are a part of "Black culture" and race shouldn't matter. Some students agreed and some disagreed. It is common knowledge that rappers use the word in their rhymes. It has an effect. Rap has been an in-your-face art form and in many ways rebellious over its lifespan. Gangster Rap (Gangsta Rap, must drop the "er" for the "a") is an example of this. I pointed out that many of the lyrics are about murdering other men, especially Black men. When rappers refer to the men they are killing, they are calling them niggas. In that instance, it does not sound like a "term of endearment."

There was also a hip-hop group from the late 1980s that my students were aware of, called N.W.A, or Niggas Wit Attitudes. I asked the students if that sounded endearing, and they obviously said no, it was more shocking. Comedians use the word a lot also. In many of their jokes, they use the word, and not as a term of endearment, as the students acknowledged. Is it OK for them to use the term? They said yes because in comedy, comedians have a public license to be funny, and can say anything they want to do their job. If you go to a comedy show, you can't be insulted. You must know where you are going and the environment you are going into. Same with a historical film, they explained. If you are going to watch a historical film on slavery, then you should not be insulted when you hear the word nigger. You willingly went to watch the movie, in similar fashion to willingly going to a comedy show where you may hear the word nigger or nigga.

I said that's great. Comedians can use the word nigga because they have a public license to do so as part of their comedy routine, and their job is to make us laugh. Got it. A White comedian can use the word nigga and there should be no problem, correct? The students had to pause. Most of the class had to seriously think about it. One student still said that White people should never use the word, even White comedians. Again, they were altering the rules. It was very confusing. There have been instances of White entertainers using both the words nigger and nigga and getting vilified by the public. I pointed out to my students that maybe they were confused as to who can or can't use it. They said they shouldn't be, that no White person can use these words or terms. In trying to understand the mindset of these young adults, I finally concluded that, in their eyes, here is who could say the word nigga: Black Americans, comedians, musicians, artists, and entertainers who are Black. Again, some in the class believe Black Americans "own" the word now. As a Black teacher, I can use the word, but it is inappropriate. And no White person should use the word, even though the word is a term of endearment.

YOUNG BLACKS VS. OLDER BLACKS

There is a clear divide about the use of the word nigga within the "Black community." Again, the course examines the different perspectives of so-called Black Americans. After discussing the thoughts on the N-Word or N-Words, the class then examined some statistics from pewresearch.org about the use of the words by Black Americans in general. According to what we saw, Black women and older Blacks were more likely to say it is never acceptable for a Black person to use the N-Word in any way shape, or form. Black men and younger Blacks tended to find it more acceptable. As pointed out earlier, when I asked one student why they don't walk up to their grandmother and call her the word nigga out of love, he responded that the word can also be used as a curse word, even though it is a greeting and a term of endearment. Surely his grandmother would not appreciate him using that word, but their friends do.

I asked the students why older adults disapprove of the word. They came up with various ideas, from the word being used by a cooler, younger generation to older Black Americans who have matured out of using the word. This is true. At 15, I might have used the word because of the influence of the music I listened to and from trying to be cool, but at 42 I may use the word less or at 62 not at all because I have grown out of it. No reason to try and be cool and impress people. I told them I understood what they were saying. I don't dress the same way that I did at age 15, so I got it.

I wanted to show them another perspective. I asked the class about older Black Americans, who may be in their 60s, 70s, 80s, etc. I asked them if, at their age, they are going through the same experiences that their grandparents went through when they were in their teens or in high school. They acknowledged that times were different. I pointed out that some of the older Black Americans who are opposed to the N-Word might not be opposed to it because they aren't "cool" or out of touch. Could it be that they are opposed to any version of the word because they came from a time when there was extreme discrimination and oppression? Could it be that they witnessed a time when the word nigger was popularly used against them in a hateful, discriminatory, and oppressive way? Could it be that the word was used in such a disrespectful manner that even just hearing the word brings back painful memories? The students acknowledged the possibility and even believed that to be the case.

I asked the students, "Is it possible that young Black Americans have had such a great life in their youth as opposed to older Black Americans had in their youth that they so willingly use the word nigga as a term of endearment whereas years ago nobody would have thought to try and take the word nigger and make it cool? Is it possible that using the term today is disrespectful to older generations of Black Americans who suffered years of abuse at the hands of the word nigger?" Something for the students to consider.

LETTING THE WORD DIE

I pointed out to the class that it is nearly impossible for a word to be used only by one community. You can't trademark its use in language, and you can never police the use of the word. If that is the case, people who they believe should never use the words nigger or nigga will use it, plain and simple. There will be people who will use it who others will feel shouldn't be using it. It will never change. The constant use of the word, whether it is the actual word or a new word derived from it, will keep it alive. We will have to just deal with the consequence that people who they do not want to use the word will inevitably use the word because many Black youth as well as music and entertainment performers keep the word or words relevant. There are pros and cons to everything. Another possibility, however, is to destroy the word. Meaning, make it so that nobody uses the word. Not in entertainment, not in movies, not in music, or anywhere else in society. This way there is no confusion. We can all understand that we can never use the word, under any circumstance. This way if anyone DOES use the word, it will now be so vile that the person who used it can be met with universal condemnation. Could we all agree to never use the word again?

As a class, they believed it was not possible as the word is so ingrained in not only "Black" American subculture, but American culture itself. The students themselves were conscious that they use the word and tried hard not to use it for one weekend. Although they made a conscious effort, and they used the word less than they had before this unit began, they still used the word. As they get older and more mature, they may use it less and eventually remove it from their vocabulary. The problem is at this rate, THEIR children may use it as THEY go to school, listen to music and watch comedians or movies, etc. (And this is not blaming any of those art forms). Musicians, entertainers, comedians, filmmakers, etc., are in the business of entertaining us and making money. If we find the use of the words nigger or nigga entertaining and they are making money from it, who should tell them not to? They are simply giving us what we want as a society if enough people want it. I doubt a comedian would walk into a church or a Buddhist temple and tell nigga jokes. If there is a desire for it in our society, and they are making money off it, then is it fair to blame them for using the word as often as they do? Do they have a moral obligation not to?

Now, that opens a whole new Pandora's box because once again. Who is determining morals or moral obligations? Truly it is up to the individual whether they want to use the N-Words, and we can never police its use. Just as in America where we believe, at least in theory, in freedom of speech, we can't control what people think or believe. How can a Black American ever stop a White American from using the word? Like it or not, the N-Words it appears, are here to stay in America. And if they do, we will always be confused as to who can use them, and in what fashion, and there will always be someone who uses them in a way that will upset others, whether right or wrong. I asked the class if Black people should stop using the N-Word. They all agreed the word nigger shouldn't be used by anyone. However, most of the class was ok with Black/African Americans using the word nigga. One student felt that word shouldn't be used either, in contrast to the rest of the class.

Questions To Consider/Answer

How do you view the words nigger and nigga? Are they the same to you? Or is there a difference?

Should either word ever be used? If so, who should be allowed to use the words, and in what capacity?

Some people believe that Black Americans have turned the N-Word, which has been negative, into a positive word. Others have argued that the use of the N-Word or N-Words is a sign of self-hate. What do you think?

Are Black/African Americans responsible TODAY *for the popularity of the N-Word through its constant usage in Black slang and entertainment? Is it the fault of Black Americans when non-Black Americans use the word? Instead of being upset with* THEM, *should Black Americans be upset with* THEMSELVES?

Do you or have you ever used the word nigger or nigga? In what capacity? BE HONEST!!!

CHAPTER SEVEN

STEREOTYPES OF BLACKS/AFRICAN AMERICANS

The class also did a unit on Stereotypes of Black/African Americans. To start the lesson, I gave the students a sheet of paper and asked them to list every stereotype they could think of about Black people. Good, bad, and ugly. You do the same. On a sheet of paper, list every stereotype of Black Americans you can think of. I told them not to hold back. I ask you to do the same. Don't be shy. I gave them 15 minutes. Many students went to the second page of the sheet because they had so many. Now that you have written down stereotypes of Black/African Americans, here is a sample of what some of my students came up with:

Sports/Rap/Fried Chicken/Grape Soda/Gangbangers/Loud/Good Dancers/Good Cooking/Violent/Sex Symbols/Watermelon/Comedians/Muscular/Big Butts/Lazy/Uneducated/Ghetto/Bad Swimmers

Of course, there were others. Many people in America, whether Black or White, would list similar stereotypes. Stereotypes are not exclusive to the "Black race." Every race or group has stereotypes associated with them. After listing the stereotypes, and having some laughs about them, we did what we always do in the class and defined the term that we were analyzing. So, what is the dictionary definition of stereotype?

Stereotype

-something conforming to a fixed or general pattern (Merriam-Webster)

-an often unfair and untrue belief that many people have about all people or things with a particular characteristic (Britannica)

-a generalization usually exaggerated or oversimplified and often offensive, that is used to describe or distinguish a group (Dictionary.com)

-a preconceived notion, especially about a group of people (Vocabulary.com)

-a stereotype is a fixed general image or set of characteristics that a lot of people believe represent a particular type of person or thing (Collins English)

We analyzed the word as a class. The students had a general idea of the definition. They understood that stereotypes apply to all people. I asked them if they stereotyped other people, and every single one of them acknowledged that they did. I asked them if THEY had ever been stereotyped, and they all again acknowledged that they had been.

I asked them to explain how they've been stereotyped. One student explained a situation where they were stereotyped in a bank. The student explained that he noticed a man walking toward him with cash when he entered the bank, and as soon as he saw the student the man went out of his way to go in an entirely different direction. I asked the student how they knew the man stereotyped him, and he said he had a feeling based on his reaction to seeing him and how quickly he avoided coming near my student. Another student explained how they felt they were stereotyped by a former teacher.

The student indicated that in one class a teacher gave them a gift card out of the blue and told the student they could use it. The student couldn't understand why and felt maybe it was because she was Black and the teacher who was White may have assumed she didn't have much money or stereotyped her as being poor. I asked the students if they stereotyped Black Americans and they all said that they did. They had a great understanding of stereotypes based on our conversation. We then went through some of the stereotypes that they came up with and tried to see why Black Americans were stereotyped or associated with the words on their lists. Each stereotype came from a total list that was created by the class together. The responses are their words on why they believed Black Americans are stereotyped in these ways.

Sports- The students explained that the stereotype of Black Americans being great at sports is because they tend to dominate popular sports in America. Sports such as football, basketball, boxing, track and field. They even pointed out that in sports that are not popular among Black Americans, Black athletes still tended to dominate, such as tennis (the Williams sisters), and gymnastics (Gabby Douglass, Simone Biles). They said that Black Americans are disproportionately successful in the sports world. (Black Americans make up 13-14% of the population and about 70-75% of the National Basketball Association at this time.) Black Americans' love of, and success at sports is why they explained, Black Americans are stereotyped as being athletic. None of my Black students in the course play a sport. They do watch sports, however.

Rap Music- Rap music or hip-hop is a musical art form created by Black youth in the inner city of New York. It is a popular form of music, and of course it is dominated by Black Americans. In fact, Black Americans are stereotyped in music far beyond rap. In general, Black Americans are considered to be great entertainers, and what is considered Black music is some of the most popular music in the world. None of the Black students in the class could rap or sing.

Fried Chicken- Ironically, my students did not understand why this stereotype was only associated with Black Americans, as all people they believed loved fried chicken. I don't know the history behind it other than to explain that in southern food, fried chicken is popular and maybe Black Americans APPEARED to disproportionately eat it as part of their cuisine. Do Black Americans traditionally love fried chicken? Sure. Do White people? Sure. Do Blacks disproportionately eat it in comparison to other groups? I have no idea. Neither did they. Has a study ever been done? My students asked if everyone loves it, why is it only associated with Black Americans? In fact, one Black student said she really didn't like fried chicken, to which we all joked "then you ain't really Black."

Grape Soda- The class stated that Black Americans are stereotyped as generally liking sweet things. Grape soda is stereotyped as being very popular among Black people. They were sure many of these stereotypes are media driven, and maybe Black Americans again disproportionately buy grape or orange soda while Asians order cola more. I have no idea. Neither did they. When I asked the class if they liked grape soda, some said yes, and others said it was too sweet.

Gangbangers- The students attributed this stereotype to the media. They acknowledged that there are Black gangs, and many of them commit murder and sell drugs. They also acknowledged that there are plenty of White, Hispanic, and Asian gangs. I pointed out to the class that one statistic states that Black Americans account for close to 80% of the murders of other Blacks in the United States according to the U.S. Department of Justice. Many of those murders are attributed to Black gangs. Many murders that occur in cities like New York and Chicago are committed by Black males. There can be some discrepancies in statistics one student mentioned. As pointed out earlier, who are they (the government and media) characterizing as "Black?" Also, how are they certain that the murder had anything to do with gang involvement? Sure, the suspect could be in a gang, but the murder of another gang member could be personal and have nothing to do with gang involvement. Splitting hairs, I understand, but Black gangs are involved in the murders of others at a high rate. The students believed that constant media attention, rap music, and movies alluding to Black gangs help to perpetuate the stereotype, as more media coverage will be given to Black gangs than to something positive like "The Black Experience in America" course.

Loud- The Black students in the course universally saw where this stereotype came from. They admitted that Black Americans are typically louder than, say, Asian Americans, for example. They said it was part of Black culture. Black people are loud. Sometimes even obnoxious. They also said the younger generation of Black Americans tended to be loud, as opposed to older generations. They even pointed out that in the hallways of the school, it was the Black students who were disproportionately the loudest.

I explained to the students that I had been guilty of stereotyping in movie theaters. When I went to see a movie many times and young Black Americans came in, I immediately started rolling my eyes expecting them to be loud. I even jokingly said that when they walked in, the movie theater should just turn on the closed caption; this way, since I wouldn't be able to hear the movie, at least I could read what the actors were saying. The class laughed, but they understood. Even in style of dress, such as sagging baggy jeans in the 1990s with underwear showing, or just general behavior, they said that young Black Americans were over the top and in your face. That is where the stereotype comes from. Black people are loud, is the class consensus. Barely any debate on this one.

Good Dancers- This is another stereotype the students understood. Black people have rhythm, was the consensus. They looked at the many Black entertainers who could dance. Michael Jackson, Beyonce, Usher, Chris Brown, etc. Some even pointed out the tribes in Africa with the drumbeats and people dancing. Watch a hip-hop music video, and most of the women dancing are Black. In contrast, the stereotype was that White people aren't good at dancing. I, as well as my students, have heard White people themselves say they have no rhythm, so it is almost as if they stereotype themselves that way.

I've heard plenty of White people say, "I have no rhythm, I'm White." (Again, how is that not racist? Are White people born with bad rhythm? Aren't they basically acknowledging that Blacks are SUPERIOR at rhythm?) There are plenty of White people who can dance, and plenty of Black people who can't. They said disproportionately in the media Black people dance, whereas you rarely see Whites or Asians doing so. I countered that there are many different forms of dancing. Black Americans might be great at break dancing, for example, but how many Black Americans do you see ballroom dancing? That could be dominated by White Americans. I don't know, but I just pointed something out. They were only focused on the style of dancing THEY preferred. However, it is a stereotype, nonetheless.

Good Cooking- Black people can cook, according to the class. They add flavor to their food. Seasoning, spices, and soul. Soul food, Caribbean food, and southern cooking are many times attributed to Black people. Soul food and southern cooking to Black Americans. Also, Black Americans are known to LOVE a good barbecue. Fried chicken, black-eyed peas, cornbread, mac 'n' cheese, chicken wings. The list goes on as far as foods that Black Americans are known for cooking. Are these foods a major part of Black American culture? That is undeniable. The students understood where this stereotype came from.

Violent- This goes back to the gang stereotype. The students acknowledged that Black Americans, particularly men, are stereotyped as being violent. A running complaint of Black men is that many women, mostly not Black, would clutch their purses when passing Black men. Where do Black men get this stereotype? Again, it could be attributed to the gang culture, or homicides committed by Black men. The students acknowledged that White people commit crimes as well but not at the rate of Black Americans, per the statistics that are given by the Department of Justice. Now, how accurate are these statistics? We couldn't possibly know.

I asked the students about fighting in school. I asked, "Who fights the most in our high school?" They said by far the Black students, particularly the Black girls. In my district currently, Black/African American students make up about 8% of the population. However, in our high school, according to the students, they made up at least 50-70% of the fights. Of course, they had no data to prove this, but they were going based on what they saw. They said these disproportionate numbers contribute to the stereotype that Blacks in America are violent. Some of the Black girls stated that Black men are known to hit and abuse their wives or girlfriends. Immediately, I challenged them.

I asked if they said this was a general stereotype or was it something that they personally believed. They said they personally believed it. I asked them if they believed I would hit my wife. Instead of answering, they asked if I had ever hit a woman. I responded, no. They replied that's rare. I asked them why they believed that most Black men hit their women. Is that not a stereotype? They mentioned that it was known in the Black community. As seen, Black people will also stereotype each other. Stereotypes can occur among members of the same group.

Sex Symbols- Another stereotype of Black Americans was over-sexualization. Black Americans are stereotyped as being oversexualized. They pointed to many hip-hop music videos showing Black women dancing provocatively. They pointed out many of the hot trends of clothing that many Black women wear. Also, some female hip-hop artists who are very popular also contribute to the stereotype, they said. Twerking, a very popular dance that is extremely sexual, is attributed to Black Americans. Even Black men are many times seen as being sexual, they said. The rhythm and dancing aspect they acknowledged also contributes to the stereotype. Another reason, I pointed out, was the reportedly high concentration of Black children born out of wedlock among Black Americans. Some may see that as Black Americans being sexually undisciplined or having no control over their sexual desires. This could be a contributing factor to the stereotype as well.

Watermelon- This is another stereotype that my students didn't understand why it was attributed to Black Americans. Who doesn't like watermelon? Ironically enough, there was a Black student in the class who did not enjoy watermelon. Again, the joke came out that they weren't Black. I showed the students a clip of a show called "Curb

Your Enthusiasm" in which a Black character secretly threw out the watermelon he was eating when he heard the White character coming. The White character discovered the half-eaten watermelon and asked the Black character why he had thrown it out, and he admitted that he couldn't eat watermelon in front of White people because he didn't want to continue to perpetuate the stereotype. The class thought it was a funny clip.

Some of the Black students admitted that sometimes they were hesitant to eat stereotypical Black foods in front of White people because they also did not want to perpetuate the stereotype. I shared experiences of White people that I was close with jokingly offering me watermelon. I also explained that this stereotype could sometimes be awkward for White people. They wondered how. I said from a White person's perspective, if they invite you to their house for a barbecue and have delicious watermelon, they may be afraid to offer it to you because they may feel they are insulting you through the stereotype. They may feel they are in a tough position. You may be in the mood for watermelon, but they may not offer it to you. We laughed about it as a class, but they could see that perspective also as some White people may not want to come off as insensitive. I explained the stereotype of Black Americans liking watermelon goes way back to the early 1900s when there were caricatures and drawings of Black Americans eating watermelon.

Comedians- Some of the most famous comedians in history are Black, the class pointed out. Among them, Richard Pryor, Eddie Murphy, Bill Cosby, Chris Rock, Kevin Hart, Dave Chappelle, Steve Harvey, D.L. Hughley, Bernie Mac, Cedric the Entertainer and so many more. Black people are funny. That was the consensus. One could argue Black Americans needed to have a great sense of humor to survive the years of discrimination and oppression that they historically have had to deal with here in the United States. There are tons of great comedians of all races. In the media, movies, etc., Black Americans appear to be disproportionately represented in this field.

Muscular- This again could go back to the sports/athletic stereotype the class pointed out. Black Americans, especially Black men, are many times stereotyped as being muscular and strong. Some may point out as some students did that many bouncers at clubs are Black men. The National Football League is mostly dominated by Black players, many of whom are huge, muscular human beings. A stereotype of teenage boys is that young, Black males tend to look older and more developed than boys of other races.

Big Butts- There were two ways to look at this. Black women are stereotyped as being naturally "curvaceous," which may add to the sexual stereotype. Black women are many times described as having curvy hips and big butts. This can go back as far as the 1800s and the exhibits of Sarah Baartman in Europe, an African woman whose body was objectified by Europeans. Many of the most famous Black female entertainers are known for their curvaceous figures, and when dancing are not afraid to show them off. The students understood and acknowledged this. They also pointed out that a disproportionate number of Black women will also do things to "enhance" their butts, which also contributes to the stereotype. Many people my age and older remember a song called "Baby Got Back" by Sir Mix A Lot, which was extremely popular in the early 1990s. Many labeled it the "Black man's anthem." Listen to the lyrics if you have never done so. It is literally a song dedicated to big butts. Surely this has contributed to the big butts and Black Americans stereotype. In fact, when a woman of ANY race has what is considered a big butt, the stereotype is a Black man will love it.

Lazy- The students noted that Black Americans are stereotyped as lazy. ESPECIALLY Black youth. I asked where this stereotype came from. I pointed out that Black Americans for years were slaves, so clearly laziness was not inherent in Black people. Also, many Black Americans since the end of slavery have worked many jobs just to make ends meet, and some even had their own successful businesses. They agreed and noted that the lazy stereotype is more recent. The number of Black people on welfare contributes to the stereotype. Black people are seen as being disproportionately on welfare in comparison with Whites and Asian Americans. In reality, from articles that we looked at online on clasp.org when analyzing this stereotype, White Americans receive the most benefits from welfare by total dollar amount and percentage. How accurate these statistics are, the class and

I could never know. I pointed out to the students that receiving welfare does not mean you are lazy. However, the stereotype of Black Americans disproportionately being on welfare is usually equated to Black Americans being lazy.

I also asked the students about Black students, and how they may contribute to the lazy stereotype of Black Americans. I pointed out that in some cases they may not have done their classwork or homework. In those classes, could they then be perceived as lazy? They said absolutely, even though that isn't fair because students of other races do the same thing. I asked if it is possible that Black students disproportionately don't do their work as much as, say, White or Asian students. They said it was possible. I explained to them that stereotypes can be based on perceptions and for many people perceptions are reality. The stereotype of Black Americans being lazy is generally attributed to Black AMERICANS. There are other "Black" people who are here in America who do not share this stereotype.

Uneducated- Black Americans have also been stereotyped as uneducated. The students pointed out the slang that Black Americans use (mostly young Black Americans), and their style of dress. I even brought up Ebonics, which was known as Black English when I was growing up, as being viewed as a dumbed-down version of standard English. I asked why Asian American students did not have this stereotype, and the class responded that Asian Americans were stereotyped as being smart. I asked why not Black Americans. They really didn't know.

I pointed out that it could also date back to the time when Blacks were enslaved in this country and the narrative was that Black slaves were uneducated, as most were. They were not allowed to go to school or learn to read. What about today when all Black children go to school? Shouldn't that stereotype have died out? Could it be that Asian American students are doing something different than Black American students? Are Asian American students born just inherently smart (again if you believe this, explain how you aren't a racist again?)? Could it be due to the BEHAVIORS of Black Americans? Could they be creating this stereotype of themselves?

Ghetto- The class mentioned that ghettos were created for Jewish people during the Holocaust in Europe, but they are not stereotyped as ghetto. According to the class, that stereotype is reserved for Black Americans. Ghettos are slums and poor areas of inner cities. The people who live there are considered very poor. Disproportionately it appears that Black Americans live in ghettos, according to the students. I pointed out to the class that when some people, White OR Black, find out that I grew up in a nice neighborhood in Long Island, they joke that I am rich. Where I grew up is as middle class as the next middle-class neighborhood.

Subconsciously these people may assume that I should have grown up poor in a ghetto and struggled. A White family in a middle-class neighborhood is seen as middle class. A Black family in the same neighborhood is seen as rich because many Americans are used to the narrative that Black Americans grow up in poor, destitute areas in inner cities. Where does this come from? Well, part of it could be that for many years Blacks were not allowed to live in nice areas. Today, the media narrative, from TV to music to movies to news networks portrays this. Black Americans also help push the stereotype by calling anything cheap "ghetto." Or telling a person that they are ghetto. It is a word that is used or that has been used in Black slang.

Bad Swimmers- My students brought up this stereotype as well. A movie called "White Men Can't Jump" starring Wesley Snipes and Woody Harrelson came out in 1992. It was a basketball movie and it played on the stereotype that White men were not as good as Black men at basketball, ESPECIALLY at jumping in basketball. I mentioned this to my students and asked them where that stereotype came from. They explained that in the NBA, the best dunkers and jumpers, from Michael Jordan to Dominique Wilkins, to LeBron James to Julius Erving, were Black. In fact, I remember the only White man to win the dunk contest, and that was Brent Barry in 1996. I was in high school. When he did it, it was revolutionary because my friends and I didn't know of White men who could jump. Most White NBA players did not attempt to dunk, it seemed, as much or as skillfully as Black players. However, the stereotype of White players is they are great shooters (Larry Bird).

As a joke about that movie, I always used to say that there should be a sequel called "Black Men Can't Swim," because one of the stereotypes of Black people is they do not know how to swim. Where does this stereotype come from? Well, historically in America, many Black children were denied access to public pools that were "White" only. In some cases, after Black people swam in the pools, the pools were drained and cleaned. Highly insulting. I explained this to the class. Around 2010, a study done by USA Swimming revealed that 70% of African American children could not swim. This is probably where the stereotype came from.

Are Black people inherently bad at swimming? Could it be a cultural reason? Is it that Blacks CAN'T swim or Blacks DON'T swim? A contributing factor TODAY that I've heard discussions about is that some Black people (Black women) in particular choose not to swim because of the damage to their hair from the chlorine. These are not my words, and I am not saying that this is why Black Americans don't swim, but it could be a contributing factor. I've never polled Black women, so it is not as if I have evidence to totally support this, but I have heard it discussed among some Black women. However, not being able to swim by choice, and not being able to swim due to a racial component, are two totally different things. Either way, it is a common stereotype of Black Americans.

HISTORY OF BLACK STEREOTYPES IN AMERICA

I went over a few historical stereotypes of African Americans that have existed in America over time. Some of the stereotypes included:

Sambo- A simple-minded, docile Black man. Popular during slavery. A Black slave happy to serve his White master

Jim Crow- An act performed at minstrel shows by White men in exaggerated dark paint and facial features performed for the entertainment of White Americans

The Savage- The Black man looking to prey on and rape White women. This gave some White people an excuse to lynch and kill Black men to protect White women.

The Mammy- An overweight Black woman who served her master in any way she could. She loved White culture even more than her own family.

Sapphire- The angry, loud, disrespectful Black woman, especially when it came to emasculating Black men. Many have argued that in present times, it is the Sapphire who damages Black men more than anyone else.

Jezebel- The beautiful and seductive Black woman who is overly sexual and appears exotic to White men.

Mandingo- A strong, muscular Black man with extreme sexual prowess who appears exotic to White women.

Pimp- A Black man with a harem of women. Made famous in blaxploitation films. Even today in Black culture, many young Black men will refer to themselves as pimps or pimpin' if they have a lot of women. My students have even referred to me as a pimp, clearly an image I am not trying to give off.

High Pain Threshold- For years it was thought that Blacks could withstand more pain than anyone else. Maybe to justify the punishments they have received since slavery.

Of course, there are many others. Now for a different perspective...

CAN STEREOTYPES BE GOOD?

I pointed out to the class that in many instances, words are just words. We are indoctrinated to think words are inherently good or bad. I asked my students if stereotypes are a good or bad thing. Universally, they said it was bad. I asked them if segregation was good or bad? Again, universally they said, bad. I then asked them would they build a school next to a jail that houses sex offenders, or would they want to "segregate" the sex offenders from the school? Obviously, they said to keep the sex offenders away from the school. I then asked them well; wouldn't that be segregation? They said yes. I then asked, in that instance, wouldn't segregation be good? They saw things from a different perspective. When some people hear the word segregation, they automatically think race, and it is a bad thing. Others may argue that segregation is a good thing by race because it prevents problems. I've heard people say that segregation is terrible, and these same people live in gated communities. Do we not want to segregate criminals from our communities? Isn't that the point of prisons? Segregation is neither a good nor bad word. It just depends on the context you use it in and on your perspective.

Stereotype is another word that could fit in that range. Once again, when I asked if stereotyping others is good or bad, the students universally proclaimed that it was bad. I gave a scenario. I asked the students if they were walking down a city street at night and saw five Black men, pants sagging, cursing, smoking weed and drinking, hanging out on a corner, would they stereotype those men? They said, probably. I asked how would you stereotype them? They said they were drug dealers or gang members. I asked, would you possibly take another street to get where you were going? Most of the students said yes. I asked in this scenario if they took another route, and then found out later that those men were involved in a shootout around the same time they changed directions, could one argue that stereotyping HELPED them avoid a problem? If we stereotype teenagers as being too immature to drink alcohol, isn't this a good thing? The students acknowledged that stereotyping in THOSE instances was a good thing but stereotyping in general is disproportionately bad.

They brought up Trayvon Martin and the stereotype of Black men wearing hoodies being negative and possibly costing Trayvon Martin his life. The class for the most part admitted that there could be times when stereotyping might be good, but usually it was a bad thing. I asked them if stereotypes are rooted in any facts about the group being stereotyped? In many cases the class admitted there had to be some truth to justify the stereotype of that group, and in many cases the stereotype is simply an exaggeration. A stereotype can be a generalization about a particular group. Generalizations don't have to be completely accurate for every single person in that group, I pointed out. I asked them if there was any way to stop stereotyping, and they said no. Stereotyping others is just a way of life we must all deal with. In the class discussion, it was explained by the students that stereotyping has had much more of a negative effect on The Black Experience in America than a positive one.

Questions To Consider/Answer

What stereotypes do you associate with Black/African Americans?

Pick any other group (racial, gender, etc....) that you stereotype or form generalizations about. What are the stereotypes for this group?

In your opinion, can stereotypes ever be a GOOD thing? If so, how? If not, why not?

Do you believe that YOU personally reinforce stereotypes (positive and/or negative) of your racial group? If so, how?

Will you continue to stereotype other groups? If yes, explain why. If not, how do you plan to stop stereotyping?

How do you think stereotypes (positive AND negative) have affected Black Americans and The Black Experience in America?

CHAPTER EIGHT

IMAGERY AND THE BLACK EXPERIENCE IN AMERICA

WHAT IS AN IMAGE?

Another topic the class discussed was imagery and how it affects the experience of Black Americans. How does what we see affect us? There was a great quote by Confucius that states, "He who controls the images, controls the minds." Images affect ALL people. How do certain images affect how others see Black Americans, and more importantly, how Black Americans view themselves? As always, we start with definitions. We looked up the word image online using standard definitions.

-a likeness of an object produced on a photographic material

-a mental conception held in common by members of a group and symbolic of a basic attitude and orientation

-a popular conception (as of a person, institution, or nation) projected especially through the mass media (Merriam-Webster)

-a physical likeness or representation of a person, animal, or thing photographed, painted, sculpted, or otherwise made visible (Dictionary.com)

-an idea, especially a mental picture of what something or someone is like (Cambridge)

-a picture or other representation of a person or thing, or it can be someone's public perception (Vocabulary.com)

-a picture that is produced by a camera, artist, mirror, etc. A mental picture, the thought of how something looks or might look (Britannica)

-a representation or likeness of a person or thing, especially in sculpture (Collins English Dictionary)

Once again, after analyzing many definitions, the class looked for similarities among them. Words that were common were pictures, and what something MIGHT look like. Another word was representation. Clearly, images are things that a person can see, whether it be with their eyes through a picture, painting, sculpture, OR what they can see mentally in the mind. How does what we see affect The Black Experience in America?

LIGHT VS. DARK IMAGES

I showed the class two different versions of Black female celebrities. In one picture, it is the celebrity in her natural state. In the other pictures, it was the celebrity on the cover of a magazine. I asked the class if they noticed anything. They sure did. When their picture was on the cover of the magazines, their complexion was far lighter than their actual complexion. Their image had been lightened. I asked the class why the magazines would do this. The class pointed out a common complaint among many Black Americans. The image of lighter skin has always been seen as more beautiful than darker skin for women. In some of the pictures, the Black female celebrities looked almost White.

I asked the class how they felt these constant images might affect young Black girls who are dark-skinned. They said this could have a negative effect, as these types of images may make them think, as well as other groups, that dark skin is not attractive. I told the students that as a teenager I would watch hip-hop music videos on TV. Many of the videos featured women dancing. Predominantly and disproportionately, the African American women tended to be fair-skinned or light-skinned. Now there were two images that stood out in these music videos that many in the Black community have complained about for years. First, many have complained that the image of Black women dancing sexually in these videos is a bad look for young females who watch these videos. Second, the women in the videos, whether they are the love interests or the dancers, usually tended to be lighter skinned. Was this a coincidence, or was this done on purpose by the directors?

Either way, I mentioned that in many cases dark-skinned women felt insulted because of the constant image of lighter-skinned females portrayed in these videos. The students knew what I was talking about. We even looked at some celebrities who at one point were dark-skinned, and over the years lightened their skin color and hair and even wore contacts that lightened their eye color. Was it the constant image of lighter skin being more desirable than darker skin? Many of my students believed this to be the case.

THE "WHITE SAVIOR" IMAGE

Another popular image that has existed in American media for years that not only Black Americans, but others of different races have complained about, is the "White Savior" image. My students were unfamiliar with this until I showed them some examples and then THEY began to give examples as well. Basically, in the White Savior image, a good-hearted White person helps or "saves" a Black person or Black people, who could not help or save themselves. Some examples that many have cited are "Diff'rent Strokes," a sitcom that ran in the late 1970s to mid-1980s in which a wealthy White man adopts two orphaned boys who come from Harlem. There was nothing wrong with the show according to many people, and the show did touch on serious issues. Another show around the same time that had a similar theme was a show called "Webster." Again, a sitcom, and nothing inherently wrong with the show. Many non-Blacks would watch the shows and see nothing wrong; however, some Black Americans have noted the point that in both cases a White family "saved" the young Black children.

They questioned why couldn't a Black family save the children. Would this not have made for good TV? Would the show be less funny or entertaining? I argued that in the early 1990s, this did occur when the "Fresh Prince of Bel-Air" debuted, in which a poor teenager from the inner city of Philadelphia moved to live with his well-off aunt and uncle in the ritzy Bel-Air neighborhood of Los Angeles. However, the response to that has been how many sitcoms have been produced where a Black family saves a White child. Why isn't this image broadcast to the American people? No right or wrong answers, but observations that have been made by some.

A couple of my students brought up the movie "Freedom Writers," (2007) and I mentioned movies including "Hardball" (2001) and "Dangerous Minds" (1995), which had similar plots. A White person works to help school-age children in one shape or another. Some Black Americans have argued that, again, this is a popular image that is shown in movies. I pointed out to my students that there are movies where a minority goes in to help minority students to excel, such as "Lean on Me" (1989) or "Stand and Deliver" (1988). In each movie, a Black man and a Hispanic man help the struggling minorities in the film. My students asked me if there are any films where a Black or Hispanic man saves a group of struggling White students. The only movie that I could think of, which I had never seen, was "To Sir, With Love" (1967) starring Sidney Poitier. It was a British film and my students had never heard of it. There were other films that I mentioned to the students in which a main point of the plot is the image of a White person who helps a Black person or people overcome a struggle. Some of the films they had heard of before and others they had not, such as:

Django Unchained(2012)

Glory Road(2006)

Blood Diamond(2006)

The Blind Side(2009)

Cool Runnings(1993)

The Air Up There(1994)

12 Years a Slave(2013)

Finding Forrester(2000)

The Help(2011)

Hidden Figures(2016)

The Legend of Tarzan(2016)

Mississippi Burning(1988)

Radio(2003)

The Soloist(2009)

Sunset Park(1996)

A Time to Kill(1996)

There are others. Some of these films are based on true stories. Many of these films are great and entertaining films. Most people will watch them, enjoy them, and go on with their lives. Some have pointed out, and as I have pointed out to my students, images can be subtle, and the constant images that people see may not be striking now but may reinforce certain things that we may not notice. White people may see these films and see nothing wrong with the images. Other White people will notice it and have an issue. Some Black people will see these films and see nothing wrong with it. Other Black people will see these films and have a problem with the constant recurrence of the White savior image, even if some of them are based on true stories. They will point out that there are a disproportionate number of these films in comparison to situations where the racial component is reversed. Who is right and who is wrong? Nobody. They are just different perspectives. Keeping an open mind to other people's views is key to this course. My students could see both sides of the coin.

THE BLACK SERVANT IMAGE

At the time of this writing, a change in two popular household brands had recently occurred. Almost every home in America has either syrup, rice, or both. Many people are familiar with Uncle Ben's Rice and Aunt Jemima syrup. An elderly black man was on Uncle Ben's Rice boxes for years. An elderly Black woman was on the front of the Aunt Jemima syrup bottle, similar to the "mammy" character discussed earlier. I asked my students if they have seen these two iconic American brands, and they said they had. We discussed the fact that many Black Americans have complained about these two images because they portray Blacks as "servants." Many people of all races never thought about this until recently, including many Black Americans. Again, images can be subtle.

I asked my students if it were possible that years and years of having these household staples in American homes could have an impact on how our minds process how people view Black Americans, including, and most importantly, how Black people view themselves. Today, Uncle Ben's Rice is now called Ben's Original, while Aunt Jemima has been renamed the Pearl Milling Company. One student didn't like the change of the names or the images, as they felt subconsciously that the products themselves had changed, but other students argued why was it necessary to have Black servants on the covers. The products are still rice and syrup.

One student pointed out that these images promote negative stereotypes of Black Americans in a very subtle way. I made sure to point out that images like this are not unique to Black Americans. I pointed out the Notre Dame Fighting Irishman, with an image of a leprechaun in a fighting stance. I asked the students if they knew of any stereotypes of Irish people, and one student pointed out that a common stereotype is that Irish people drink, get drunk at bars, and fight. I asked, "Do you believe this image helps to fuel this stereotype?" The student answered yes. I asked if they had ever heard Irish people complain about it. They said no but that does not mean there aren't Irish people who do not have an issue with it. People in a particular group can have different perspectives on the same subject.

IMAGERY AND BLACK CHILDREN

When it comes to images as they relate to children, specifically Black children, times are changing. Take Disney characters, for example. When I was a child, most Disney princesses were White. It was so normalized that many people didn't even notice. I showed the class popular Disney princesses from the 1980s and 1990s. Snow White, Ariel, Cinderella, Sleeping Beauty, Rapunzel, and so on. Some saw this as a constant image of princesses and royalty being reserved for White women. How might a young Black girl interpret these images? Disney is popular among children of ALL races. Today, however, Disney has attempted to offer different perspectives of princesses to be more inclusive of children of other races. I pointed this out to the class.

Princess Jasmine was popular when I was a child. She was not traditionally White. Today, many of my students point to a variety of different Disney princesses, such as Pocahontas, Mulan, and Princess Tiana, a Black princess. The class clearly believed that Disney noticed the imagery of what they were portraying and tried to change it. Staying with the Disney theme, we looked at a popular movie from the 1990s called "The Lion King." To most people, it is just a cartoon. Again, many things that we take for granted are littered with subtle images and imagery that can affect the mind. I pointed out to the class the appearance of the lions in the film. The good Lion Mufasa was light. The evil lion "Scar" was dark. Some Black Americans had an issue with this. Why couldn't the good lion be dark, and the evil lion be light? What does this image, as subtle as it may be, portray? A White person may not see an issue there, while a Black person might. Again, different perspectives. The class as a whole saw what the issue could be.

Superhero images today are vastly different than they were 20 to 30 years ago. Today you have the hit film "Black Panther." Many adults today my age will tell you that most of the images of the heroes we saw looked nothing like us. Batman, Spiderman, and Superman were all White. He-Man was White. And there are others. In fact, there was a cartoon called ThunderCats that I loved as a child. I pointed out to the class that my friends and I, who were Black, theorized that Panthro the panther cat was Black because he sounded Black. It gave us someone to relate to. Times have changed, however, as there has been a Black Spiderman and Batman. Not as popular as their White counterparts but still an effort has been made to display different images. Most people do not believe these images were displayed on purpose this way to children to create a positive or negative mindset in children. Some people believe they were. Living in a White majority society these images would be slanted toward a White majority society. However, the class acknowledged that the images, whether done intentionally or not, still would have an impact on children.

One student even brought up Barbie dolls, which again for the most part have been dominated by White Barbie dolls. There are Black Barbies as well, but the student pointed out that they only had White Barbies as a child as the Black Barbies were much harder to find. She pointed out that many Black children had grown accustomed to playing with White Barbies and thought nothing of it. The student then asked how many White children had grown accustomed to playing with Black Barbies. The student pointed out that in a country where most people claim they are not racist or "don't see color," she believes that most White families do not own Black Barbies at the same rate that a Black family will own White Barbies. Of course, I have no evidence or stats to say which families own which Barbies.

We also discussed Santa Claus. My students know Santa to be White. Every Christmas, parents of ALL races bring their children to meet Santa Claus or discuss Santa Claus with their children. Santa Claus is responsible for bringing good children their gifts. No harm, right? What is the IMAGE of this Santa Claus? A student pointed out that it was nearly impossible to find a Black Santa Claus anywhere. Why can't Santa Claus be Black? Why can't he be Mexican? Why can't he be Japanese? After all, he is make-believe, isn't he? It isn't like the students were asking for a Black Princess Diana when Princess Diana was actually White. Some students argued that since Santa is make-believe and doesn't really exist, there should be multiple versions of Santa Claus. What would be the problem, they asked? One student, however, had no issue with a White Santa Claus and felt it should be left as is.

Some students had an issue with Black parents who work hard to provide gifts for their children only to have their children buy into the IMAGE that a White Santa Claus gave them the gifts. They argued that this subtle image may make Black children think less of their parents and look up more to a White person. They also questioned how many White parents would bring their child to a Black Santa in the same manner that Black parents are open to bringing their children to a White Santa. They brought up the point that in a nation where many people claim to never see color, or that racism doesn't exist, why would anyone have a problem with more multicultural Santa Clauses'? If Black parents can willingly take their children to see a White Santa and believe in a White Santa Claus (as every child in the class grew up believing), then White parents and their children should have no problem taking their children to a Black Santa Claus. One student, however, felt that Santa's race should not matter. It is made up for children, even though the student did acknowledge the image issue that could arise from it. However, some other students pointed out that the imagery starts from a young age and can INDOCTRINATE people. As stated earlier, indoctrination starts young. Both sides may have been making a very valid point. Again, questions open the mind to thinking. The students were questioning the images they had seen since they were extremely young.

"WHITE" JESUS

Another image that was discussed at great length by the students was the image of a "White" Jesus. As an activity, and you can do the same, we googled Jesus Christ and clicked on the images. Every image that appeared was an image of a "White" Jesus. Flowing blond hair and beard in some sort of robe or on the cross during his crucifixion. Nobody alive can accurately tell you what Jesus Christ looked like. Anyone who tells you they know exactly what Jesus looked like is lying. The class agreed to this. The question they wondered about was why was there a consensus that Jesus looked this way? Why do most churches have this IMAGE of Jesus? Is it even accurate? Also, how might this image impact people who DON'T look like the image of Jesus that is constantly portrayed? Indeed, images of Jesus as a White man are all throughout the world from paintings to pictures to portraits. So where does this come from, the students asked?

For one thing, I explained to the students that the Bible makes almost no mention of Jesus' appearance. One student mentioned that there was a verse in the Bible that alluded to Jesus having hair like wool and feet of brass. In other parts of the world, images of Jesus have been drawn to reflect the appearance of the people who live in that region but the image of Jesus as White is still very popular. In America, the images of Jesus are almost universally White. In fact, we googled "Black" Jesus Christ and found very few images. The class observed that googling Jesus Christ brought up images of a White man, but you had to google "Black Jesus Christ" to get any images of Jesus as a Black man, so they argued that there was a clear bias in place. One student, however, did say that in the church they sometimes attend they have images of a Black Jesus, but the student believed this to be rare.

One of the students had a serious issue with Black churches in America (another topic discussed in the course) as they believed that Black churches helped to promote the image of a White Jesus. The student argued that if Jesus were actually White, they would have no problem with the image, however, we do not know what Jesus looked like and besides, in the region of the world that he came from at the time, people had brown skin. He could not have possibly had blond hair and blue eyes as most of the people in that region at the time had brown skin and brown eyes. The student pointed out that Christianity is one of the world's largest religions and Christians worship Jesus Christ as God.

If Black people are worshiping the image of a White Jesus, then by default they are worshiping a White God which, going back to the days of slavery, reinforced the inferiority of Black people in relation to Whites. The students pointed out that Black churches have also pushed this narrative by placing a false image of a White Jesus in their churches. Also, many Black Americans will eagerly hang up a picture of a White Jesus in their home. The student then questioned how many White people or White churches would eagerly put up an image of a Black Jesus in their church, since once again many Americans claim not to see color or that racism doesn't really exist. The rest of the class agreed with her.

Should Jesus' race matter? I asked the class this question. I asked if it were more important to focus on the MESSAGE of Jesus as opposed to the IMAGE of Jesus. If you follow the teachings of Jesus, you will know that Jesus preached or taught love and humility for and of all people. Forgiving others and doing kind deeds. I asked the class, shouldn't that be the focus of Jesus, not the way he looks? Members of the class agreed but unfortunately, the world doesn't see things that way.

The same student from earlier also pointed out that some churches have been known to abuse their power and use their power to INDOCTRINATE and control people. My students remembered their history, as this is true and has been true throughout history even up to the present. Again, they pointed to the image of a White Jesus as a way to control and indoctrinate Black Americans into believing that their God was a White man. The same student acknowledged again that had Jesus been White and we knew that for a fact, they would have no problem with it. However, since we have no idea what he looked like AND factually speaking the Jews in Galilee where Jesus was from had predominantly brown skin and brown eyes, then it absolutely matters what image is being portrayed of Jesus, especially if it is inaccurate.

The students reiterated that the image of Jesus matters because, in their estimation, most White people in America would have a problem hanging up a Black Jesus in their homes or churches at the same rate that Black Americans have hung up a White Jesus in their homes and churches for years. If the image of Jesus does not matter, then why is there the same constant image of Jesus repeatedly? They did not believe it was a coincidence and one student argued the image was crafted on purpose.

IMAGES ON TELEVISION AND IN MEDIA

I showed the students historical images of Black Americans. From offensive cartoons to offensive drawings to offensive toys, I showed them some of the items that for years existed in America that they would not be familiar with today because these images are considered awful. There was a time during American history when these things were acceptable. I am sure there are similar things for members of other groups, as I pointed out to the class, but again we are trying to look at different perspectives through the eyes of Black Americans. I asked the class how they feel about the image of Black Americans in television and media.

The students for the most part believed it to be negative. They felt Black Americans are portrayed disproportionately in stereotypical ways. Some students believed that the images given of Black Americans usually portrayed an image of poverty, violence, hypersexuality, or as entertainers. I pointed out that many television shows historically portrayed Black families as struggling to get by. I also pointed out, however, that over time things started to change in the way Black American families were portrayed. "The Jeffersons" showed one example of a Black family that became prosperous in America. As a child, I remembered "The Cosby Show," which really hit home, about a Black American family that was successful and portrayed Black Americans in a positive way. "A Different World" was a show about Black college students that was a spin-off of "The Cosby Show." You also had shows such as "Family Matters" and "The Fresh Prince of Bel-Air" that portrayed strong, independent Black families, so things had changed over time.

There are more positive images of Black Americans today as opposed to 60 years ago.

I wanted to make sure that they saw both sides of the coin. These shows today are shown in reruns but back when I was young, they were on the air for the first time. I asked them if they thought the class "The Black Experience In America" was something positive, not only for Black Americans but for all Americans and they said, absolutely. I asked them if they believed the course will ever be promoted in the media. They said it was possible, however, they had their doubts. What do you think? Most positive things are not promoted in the media, ESPECIALLY when it comes to Black Americans, which was the class's consensus.

I asked the students whose fault it was that the media disproportionately portrays Blacks in a negative image. They said the media at first, but then I challenged them. I asked them if Black Americans should take some of the blame as well. They had to think about it. The question led to the next topic discussed in this book. Either way, most members of the class believed that negative images that Black Americans have seen over the course of history may have negatively impacted the behaviors and thought processes of Black Americans disproportionately. What do you think?

Questions To Consider/Answer

What impact do you believe images can have on a group of people, positive and/or negative?

How have the images you have seen over the course of your life impacted the way you think or view things in society?

Do you believe the image of Jesus' race matters? Why/Why not? If you practice Christianity, would you be comfortable putting up an image of a Jesus that did not look like you?

Do you believe it is important for children to see different images of characters they look up to? Why/Why not?

Do you believe the images portrayed of Black/African Americans have been generally positive or negative? Who is responsible for this in your opinion?

CHAPTER NINE

BLACK AMERICAN CULTURE: WHAT IS IT?

Another heavily debated topic in the course was Black American culture. This was a tough topic because it is hard to define Black American culture. There were so many ways to go with this topic. Of course, we had to define the term we were focusing on, which was culture. My students knew the definition, of course, but we still looked it up. So, what is the definition of culture?

-the customary beliefs, social form, and material traits of a racial, religious, or social group (Merriam-Webster)

-the sum of attitudes, customs, and beliefs that distinguishes one group of people from another (Dictionary.com)

-the beliefs, customs, arts, etc., of a particular society, group, place, or time (Britannica)

-a particular society or civilization, especially considered in relation to its beliefs, way of life or art (Collins English Dictionary)

To keep things simple, the class defined culture as the way of life of a group of people. This way of life encompasses everything they practice and believe in, from food to style of dress to religious beliefs to musical form, etc. We were going to attempt to analyze Black American culture and how it relates to The Black Experience in America. Easy, right? Do all Black Americans have the same or similar culture? That is what many people in America, including some Black people, believe. However, I pointed out a major problem in trying to analyze Black American culture. Can there ever be a consensus among Black people on Black American culture?

AFRICAN CULTURE VS. CARIBBEAN CULTURE VS. BLACK AMERICAN CULTURE

The first issue that many non-Black Americans and some Black Americans don't even realize when speaking of "Black culture" is that there are different "Black" cultures in America. There are Black people in America whose families come straight from Africa. There are Black people in America whose families come from the Caribbean or the West Indies. There are Black people in America whose families are direct descendants of slaves who were forcefully brought to America. I pointed this out to the class, and they acknowledged this. I explained to the class that my family is from the island of Barbados in the Caribbean. My parents immigrated to this country in the 1970s, so I am a first-generation American. I had another student whose grandparents came from the Caribbean as well. What most non-Black people do not realize is that there is a difference between Black people raised in African Culture vs. Caribbean Culture vs. Black American Culture. Although considered "Black" here in America, these different cultures have had issues in the past.

I was born in Brooklyn, New York, and grew up in a predominantly West Indian community until I moved to Westbury, Long Island, a suburb of New York City. My new friends would remark that I sounded different. In Westbury, I had a mix of friends who were raised in Caribbean households, African households, and Black American households. Today, I have friends who are immersed in a blend of African and American culture, Caribbean and American culture, and Black and American culture. I have seen people in African culture here in America wearing a style of dress I would never dream of wearing. Even within my Caribbean roots, the language and dialect are completely different from the language and dialect spoken on the island of Haiti, for example. When my friends said I spoke or sounded different, they were alluding to a slight accent I probably had when I moved from Brooklyn.

I shared stories with my students about how my friends and I discussed how we were punished by our parents. The African and Caribbean parents punished their children much more harshly than the Black American parents. It also appeared that the African and Caribbean parents were stricter, as their children found it much harder to do things that Black American children were allowed to do. There have been clashes between the subgenres of Black Americans as many Black people born in America have complained that African and Caribbean Black Americans have looked down on them as lazy or weak-minded.

I pointed out that many Blacks raised in African or Caribbean Black culture focus much less on slavery as opposed to Black Americans of American Black culture. When I began the topic of Black culture, I asked the students to tell me what they thought about Black culture. They were a little confused, so they asked me what exactly I meant by Black culture. They said it could mean a lot of different things. I agreed and told them that was the point. I wanted them to tell me what automatically came to their mind when I said Black culture, without guiding them. I wanted it to be a natural reaction.

What do you think of Black culture? How would you describe it? They mentioned that there were different "types" of Black Americans, to which I agreed, and three students mentioned Black Americans who could be African or Caribbean. One of my Hispanic students brought up Black Americans of Hispanic culture. I encouraged them to write down what came to mind when they thought about Black Americans and the culture that they feel is associated with Black Americans in general. The entire class acknowledged that there were many subgenres of "Black culture." They also laughed at the notion that all Black people share the same culture. I gave the students 20 minutes to write down their description of Black culture. You do the same. What is your description of Black culture? Whatever you associate with it.

COMMON ADJECTIVES OF BLACK CULTURE

Of course, the students had varied responses. A few students believed that Black American culture was the foundation for most things that were considered "cool" or "trendy." They mentioned Black music, Black entertainment, and even Black hairstyles. Some students mentioned that Black American culture was underappreciated in America for its contribution to overall American culture. Even Black slang and style of speaking, they said, played a major role in overall American culture. I guess on this point you could argue it is valued, going back to the class discussion on the usage of the word nigga among members of all races, which many students in my class claimed Black Americans now owned.

One student mentioned other aspects or adjectives brought up with Black culture. They mentioned drugs, gangs, murder, and violence as being part of Black culture, along with the other things that were mentioned by the other students such as music, style, creativity, and entertainment. One student said that everybody loves Black culture, but I challenged them. I asked them if they were sure about that statement, that EVERY American loved Black American culture. The student had to rethink it. I pointed out that there may be Black Americans who themselves might not like Black culture, or what is associated with Black culture. From the viewpoint of the class, they mostly had an overwhelmingly positive attitude toward Black American culture and felt it was great.

A major component of the class is to challenge the students to see things from a different perspective. And one student had already started that process of looking at things from a different viewpoint. Clearly, Black American culture has had a TREMENDOUS impact on Blacks in America AND America as a whole. Over time, culture can change. I asked the class what if I told you that Black American culture today is detrimental to Black Americans, and can be seen negatively in some ways? It piqued their curiosity. I showed them a CNN article from 2014 about Black culture. The students read the article and the class came to a consensus on how we should look at Black culture for the purpose of discussion. We would use a phrase from the article as our "definition" of Black culture since it was virtually impossible to define because of all the various aspects associated with it. The article pointed out that:

"Black Culture is a lifestyle standard made of assumptions about Black identity, often used successfully by marketers, studio heads, fashion brands and music labels to make money. It can be a "cool factor" that makes kids line up for hours to spend their last dime on brand new Michael Jordan sneakers. Or the thing that makes White people call me "brotha" and blast 2Chainz when I hop in the car. IT'S WHAT PEOPLE ASSUME ABOUT Black people AND HOW THEY SHOULD LIVE AND ACT."

-*Justin Simien, 5 Things to Know About Black Culture Now*

The last sentence really stood out. Black Culture is what most Americans assume or think or associate with Black people. There were many aspects of Black culture that the class could discuss, so we chose to discuss things that the students found most interesting. To begin, I asked them, when people think of Black culture, in general, do they focus more on the older generation of Blacks like their grandparents, the middle generation of Blacks like their parents, or younger generations of Blacks of their age? They all agreed that Black culture today is mostly associated with their younger generation. Therefore, we found it relevant to discuss things they would be interested in. We could spend hundreds and hundreds of pages on Black culture in this book and we could have spent a whole semester on just Black culture in the class. In the interest of time, we will focus on a couple of discussions the class had in relation to Black culture.

BLACK CULTURE AND DATING

If you recall your high school years, dating may have been very important. The dating culture of young Black students was a hot topic. For fun, I asked the students to talk about the ideal person they wanted to date and eventually marry. There were two boys in the class, both Black, and their responses were generic. They only cared if the girl they would date/marry was good-looking and nice. They were simple. If you're a heterosexual man reading this, what would you look for in a girl when you were dating in your 20s (the students were 16 and 17)? The girls' conversation about dating was extremely interesting.

As a reminder, the class had eight students. Six girls and two boys. Nine if you counted a girl (Black) who was not officially in the class but regularly sat in on it. When we started to discuss dating, the girls were very specific, ESPECIALLY the BLACK girls. We decided to have some fun. We went online, and I showed the class a dating calculator I had heard of for women. It allowed the user, a female, to input her ideal man, the man she expected to be with or desired, and it gave her the odds that she would find this man using the entire U.S. population and eliminating men based on their descriptions and statistics of the American population. Is this calculator 100% accurate? Most things are not; however, it is a good tool to give a person a gauge to look at and reanalyze their way of thinking.

We decided that each female student in the class would get an opportunity to describe the ideal man she wanted to end up with, input the information in the calculator, and then see the likely percentage that they would find this man. The class had three Black girls, two Hispanic girls, and one Native American girl. The calculator figured out its computation based on the most basic characteristics of a man, such as race, age, height, weight (could he be overweight or not), and income. The girls were extremely excited to see their percentage. Each girl got a chance, and the class noticed something that tends to be all too common among many young Black girls and women. The Black girls all wanted the same type of man. For race they only wanted Black men. They wanted men over 6'2" tall, not overweight, and between the ages of 20-26. They wanted men making more than $100,000 a year.

The non-Black girls, however, described the man they were comfortable ending up with as being any race, under 6' tall, he could be overweight, ages 20-30 (the calculator started at the age of 20), and making as little as $30,000-$70,000. A clear difference. The calculator spit out the likely percentage that they would meet these ideal men. Each of the Black girls' percentage of meeting these men was well under 1%. In fact, they were in extremely low decimals such as 0.0002 percent, on average. However, the non-Black girls in the class ranged from 3% to one girl being as high as 30%. To really drive the point home of the difference between the Black girls and non-Black girls, I asked Black girls and Hispanic girls that I knew in other classes who I had a good rapport with if they would be interested in doing the same activity and they were VERY interested.

Again, the Black girls I asked all wanted Black guys over 6' tall (6'4" was considered ideal), all with an athletic build, no overweight men, making at least $90,000 a year. However, the Hispanic girls I asked picked any race, all wanted men under 6' tall (some went as low in height as 5'5"), wanted men up to the age of 27-28 and said the man only needed to make $50,000-$80,000 a year. Again, their chances of meeting the man they wanted were much higher than for the Black girls. I also asked three White female students and they were similar in preference to the Hispanic girls. Their percentages ranged around 2%.

Back in my class, we decided to analyze this. The girls wanted to know why the likelihood of finding their ideal man was so low. I broke it down for them. As of the year 2020, there are around 330 million Americans. Black Americans make up about 13%-14% of the population. There are more Black women than Black men in America so since the Black girls ONLY wanted Black men, the highest percentage they could have was around 6%. Also, age factored in as well. Since the girls were 17 or 18 years old, they stayed in the 20–25-year-old age range. I had to ask them how many 20-year-olds make $100,000 annually. How many men of any age in America make $100,000 a year? They also wanted men over 6' tall. The average height of a man in America currently is around 5'10". I could not find an accurate statistic on average Black male income in America, but we did find that Black household income on average was under $100,000 a year, so that also affected the Black girls' percentage. According to a CNBC article from July 18, 2020, titled "Here's how much men and women earn at every age", the average Black man in the age group that the Black girls desired was under $30,000. Finally, as of 2018, 70.6% of Black men were overweight or obese, so that also greatly affected their percentages. Not to mention that married men were excluded, so the girls would not have access to those men.

Based on their preferences, they chopped off most men in every single category. We got our information from two websites, Blackdemographics.com and minorityhealthhhs.gov. I asked the class why there was such a disparity between the choices of the Black and non-Black girls. I asked them what was more of a driving factor in the disparity in dating: race or culture? They acknowledged it was culture and not race, as Black girls are not inherently born with the instinct to want a man making $100,000 a year, for example. Also, we acknowledged that not EVERY Black girl or Hispanic or White or Asian girl is looking for the same exact thing in a man, but there can be patterns that develop because of a particular culture, and there are many subcultures within a culture.

So why do so many Black American girls DISPROPORTIONATELY prefer tall men who make a lot of money, are in good physical shape, and are Black? Why were they so attracted to this? They said they need a man who made money, and they like tall men, but I asked again if this is an inherent attraction. I asked whether it could be the culture that they associate with. They started looking at things differently as they admitted that they were not born with these preferences. One Black girl, when talking about the man she wants to be with, always mentioned a man who was in the NFL or NBA. I asked why they didn't look for engineers or doctors or teachers, and she said that was "boring." What type of characteristics are common to men who play in the NBA or NFL? Tall, athletic, Black, and rich. She is not the only Black girl who wants to end up with an athlete. Are Black men stereotyped or imagined as being engineers, doctors, or teachers? We know the answer to that. And yes, women of all races may desire NBA and NFL athletes, but it seems to be disproportionately high among Black girls and women in their late teens and 20s. Why is this?

I asked the class if Black culture could be rooted in stereotypes and images that the students have been constantly bombarded with over the years? Again, the stereotype of Black men is that they are athletic, and many are athletes. Professional athletes are perceived as making a lot of money. Black girls who see these images and stereotypes bring them into their culture, and this is what they prefer. On the other hand, Hispanic men are not stereotyped as NBA or NFL players. Could it be that in their culture, Hispanic women are looking for something different and therefore height and salary aren't as important? If Asian men are stereotyped as doctors and engineers, is it possible that Asian women disproportionately prefer men who are doctors and engineers?

Another statement that was common among the Black girls was that they wanted a man to "protect" them. When I asked what that meant, they said a man who can fight and "throw down," or "get active." Again, what is another stereotype or image of Black men? Violent and aggressive. I asked the girls, if you need protection so much, who the hell is trying to kill you? The class laughed. As a Black man, I have heard a disproportionate number of Black women say they need a man to "protect" them. I am always wondering, protect them from what? Do White, Hispanic, and Asian women say this when they are looking for a man? Maybe. Do they say it as much as many Black girls do? The class acknowledged they didn't think so.

I also questioned why the students only thought of protection as fighting. If a man provides a home or gets a life insurance policy in case he dies to financially take care of or "protect" you, or builds a stock portfolio for you, is this not protection? The Black girls in my class had never looked at it from that perspective. They only looked at it in the form of violence. I asked the class if many Black women are always looking for a man to protect them physically, could this be one of the reasons that the murder rate in the Black community is higher than in other racial communities in the United States? Another common theme among the Black girls was having "fun" in their 20s. I asked them what exactly that meant. They basically said going to college, partying, and enjoying their 20s. I asked them if they were looking to have a "hot girl summer," a popular phrase in Black culture empowering young (and some old) women, mainly Black to have a wild time (usually in the summer).

Next, I decided to show the class some statistics I wanted them to analyze and give me their opinions on. Using Blackdemographics.com once again, we looked at Black marriage in America. We saw a disturbing trend. As of 2019, only 30% of African Americans were married. Black Americans were the least-married group in the United States. Asian Americans were the highest. Also as pointed out to the students, Asian Americans have the highest household income in the United States. Coincidence? According to the website, it showed that 52% of Black men were never married, and 48% of Black women were never married. Again, high percentages, and the highest of any racial group.

Are Black people racially inherently against marriage, OR could there be something in recognized Black CULTURE that is fueling this? Could it be the desires of Black men AND women based on their "cultural preferences?" The girls started to analyze their preferences and relate them to the likelihood of getting married. If Black men and women only base marriage on materialistic things, could this hurt Black people when it comes to the culture of marriage? Are young Black men looking for a type of girl based on perceived Black culture that makes it harder for THEM to find a mate? Again, we don't have answers, just questions. Clearly, there is something off in Black culture that marriage rates are low unless Black Americans don't value marriage. Do Black people, as part of their culture, just not want to get married? Maybe, maybe not. I asked the girls in the class if they wanted to get married. They all said yes. I asked the boys, who are both Black, and they were indifferent. They said maybe. No hard answers, but just questions. The girls admitted they wanted to reanalyze their dating preferences. They didn't say they would necessarily change them.

BLACK CULTURE, SCHOOL, AND EDUCATION

As mentioned earlier, when it comes to culture the choices are infinite as far as discussion is concerned, so we looked at subjects that pertain directly to the students in the class. We next looked at Black culture and school, specifically the "Black culture" of our specific high school and high schools in America in general. I asked the students if Black students valued school and education. The students admitted, not to the degree that they should. As with most high schools in America, students in my school have fights and altercations. I asked the students what group of students have the most fights in schools. Without hesitation, they said the Black students. I asked the students what group is in the hall the most after the bell rings for class. Again, they said the Black and Hispanic students. I asked them which group of students gets suspended the most for actions and behavior. They said the Black students.

Currently, in my high school, Black students are the third highest "racial" group, yet, according to my students, disproportionately account for most fights, altercations, suspensions, and being late to class. I didn't ask the school for the statistics of fights, late arrivals, etc. so we didn't know if the students' beliefs were facts. I asked the class if Black students are inherently inferior at getting to class on time, or behaving themselves, or not getting suspended. The class knew that was ridiculous. Before I could ask, they related it to Black culture in the school.

I pointed out that when people on the outside of our school and many other schools that have a similar issue with Black students see the number of suspensions of Black and Hispanic students, it could be taken that the school is racist (discriminatory) against those two groups. I asked the class their thoughts. They said in some instances, discrimination plays a part, and in others it doesn't. I asked them about our school, and the students did not believe for the most part that the suspensions and disciplines handed down on the Black and Hispanic students were solely discrimination. They acknowledged most of it was due to behavior; HOWEVER, they did say there are instances where prejudice and bias may have led to a Black or Hispanic student being punished when they really should not have been. Overall, they said it was the behavior of many Black students in the school that contributed most.

So why do the Black students fight so often (not to say that all they are doing is fighting in school. Just according to the students, it is disproportionate)? In many cases, the problems stem from outside the school setting on social media, the students told me, and usually, the students don't see each other UNTIL they are in school. One student said that when a student talks about another student in an offensive way it makes them want to fight. I asked if students talking about each other was only done by Black students. Don't White students talk about each other offensively as well? Why aren't they fighting in school at the same rate as Black students? The class had no real answer. Could it be the culture of the Black students in our high school as well as other schools as well? Maybe, maybe not. No right or wrong answers.

Next, I asked the class if they saw me as being successful. Hard question to answer, but they said yes, they would look at me as successful(I am not saying that I am successful). However, if I asked them to name successful people, who might they think of? Again, most of the students alluded to either a professional athlete OR an entertainer. I asked them why they wouldn't say a teacher, or a doctor, or an engineer. What is the fascination with sports among young Black people? Why do many Black girls want to date an athlete, yet completely ignore the quiet AP student? Again, this isn't just Black girls, as the class pointed out, but they did acknowledge that, disproportionately, most Black girls will not go for the "geeky" kids. In Black culture, they said that geeks are considered "corny." I asked if the Black students in the high school looked up to me as a "successful" Black man because I am a Black teacher. The class acknowledged that they believed many do, but more need to.

I asked if a Black, successful engineer was giving a lecture in the auditorium, or a famous rapper was doing the same, who would more kids go to listen to and of course, they picked the rapper. Engineering is boring, the students pointed out (except one student who wanted to be an engineer). I argued that the average engineer probably makes more money than the average rapper, so why would you want to hear what a rapper had to say over an engineer? Again, they said engineering is boring. I asked what is it about Black AMERICAN culture that does not put an emphasis on education as much as other cultures? Black African culture in America sure does. Why does it seem that Black students disproportionately focus more on sports than their academics according to their theories? Why does the athlete who can dunk a basketball get more love and recognition than the student who is in advanced college classes in high school getting straight A's? Why do so many Black parents look at athletics as a way out of tough situations rather than education? Why do many Black parents spend hours practicing catching a football or dribbling a basketball, but not the same number of hours doing math and science with their children?

Students acknowledged that this behavior was disproportionate in Black AMERICAN culture. The NBA has between 400-500 players in the entire league. Yet I showed the class different studies that say there are between 200,000 to 2 million engineers in America. Why don't more African American students focus on science, math and technology? Not saying there aren't Black students who don't, but by proportion, it doesn't seem as if they do according to the class. Is this accurate? What do you think? Do Black students overwhelmingly go into these studies, and it is just not advertised? Isn't it more likely that our children will become successful engineers than NBA players? Why spend so much time on something that is highly unlikely? Is an engineer or a doctor or a teacher or a scientist not successful? I once heard from an Asian American that in his culture, his parents focused strictly on math and science, and expected him to become a doctor or engineer. Not sports. Again, in 2021, Asian Americans have the highest household income in America as several studies have shown(pgpf.org). Is this due to their "race" or "culture," I asked the students. You can probably guess the class response by now. Is this a coincidence? Maybe, maybe not. What do you think?

THEY AINT REALLY BLACK

Many will tell you that Black culture is based on race, but others will say it is not based on race in many respects. On the one hand, "Black culture" is related to "Black people." If a person can freely choose their racial identification according to the United States Census, who really is a part of Black culture? Is it really based on a person's race? Black people are not a monolithic group, so it is hard to identify Black culture. Black culture is simply rooted in stereotypes and images that are portrayed of "Black people" mostly by the media and in society.

Something that has been common for years in America, is when a Black person is labeled as not being "Black." Earlier in the book when discussing stereotypes, I told a student that they weren't really "Black" because they didn't like fried chicken or watermelon. It was an obvious joke, and we had a good laugh about it. When not used as a joke, it can be HIGHLY insulting to Black Americans. A student in the class who is African American stated that they had been told they weren't really "Black." I asked the student why they believed that they were labeled by some as not being "Black?" I asked the student if they considered themselves Black and the student said yes, absolutely. So why did some people tell them that they weren't "really Black?" For one, the student spoke "well" was the response. They were articulate. The student was very fair-skinned (I guess for a Black person? Again, is there a color guide to determine Blackness?). The student planned to be an engineer. The student lived in a nice neighborhood. And they didn't sound like a "typical Black person." In fact, the student said that many times they were told that they "talked" or "sounded" White by both Blacks and non-Blacks.

Two students in my class would joke with this student (saying he wasn't really Black because he had never eaten collard greens, which I guess is considered a part of Black American culture). However, I pointed out to one of the two students that they admitted they don't eat watermelon or fried chicken so they must not be a part of Black culture either. That student had a hard time seeing it that way (a clear bias). Also, if an Asian man eats fried chicken and collard greens as his favorite meal, does that make him a part of Black culture? The student said that other Black people would tell him he wasn't really Black because he didn't fit the stereotype or image of a Black person's culture.

I asked the class if this was insulting, and they said absolutely. I also asked them if they had ever used that phrase toward another Black person in earnest and some of them said yes. I asked the class if using that phrase is not only insulting to the person they are using it toward but also to themselves if they are Black also. They asked how. I explained that one of the many gripes of Black Americans is that non-Blacks think that we are all the same, but then some Black Americans will turn and criticize another Black American for being different. Here's an example. Try being a Black Republican in the United States of America. Good luck.

Many Black Republicans, especially those who are outspoken, have been labeled as being not really Black, or "Uncle Toms," which is another highly insulting term. If Black Americans are not all the same, why would we expect all Black people not to vote Republican? Are Black Republicans not a part of Black Culture? Why not? Many Black Americans will exclude them from Black culture. A Black conservative or a Black Republican in America will tell you the struggles they deal with in their relationships with many Black Americans. I pointed this out to the class. How does one qualify for being a part of "Black culture?" It was hard for the class to answer.

As an activity, I had the class fill out a "Who is Black" checklist. I asked the class to rate and score three different people and rate who was "Blacker." I ask you to fill out the same rating scale. For each description of the person, answer yes or no if the action or adjective about them would make them Black or a part of Black culture according to the majority of Americans, ESPECIALLY young Black Americans. Tally up all the yes votes, add them and that will tell you which person was "Black" and which person "ain't Black."

Using the following checklist, determine if <u>Billy</u> belongs to "Black Culture":

He is Black	Y	N
He isn't into basketball or sports	Y	N
He is a Republican	Y	N
He wants to be a biologist	Y	N
He grew up in the Beverly Hills	Y	N
He was raised by both parents	Y	N
He has never been in a fight	Y	N
He likes country music	Y	N

He hates hip-hop	Y	N
He loves science fiction	Y	N

Using the following checklist, determine if <u>Tyrone</u> belongs to "Black Culture":

He is Black	Y	N
He is good at multiple sports	Y	N
He is a Democrat	Y	N
He wants to be a rapper	Y	N
He grew up in the projects	Y	N
He was raised by his mom	Y	N
He fights all the time	Y	N
He speaks in slang	Y	N
He loves fried chicken	Y	N
He loves BET (Black Entertainment TV)	Y	N

Using the following checklist, determine if <u>Michael</u> belongs to "Black Culture":

He is White	Y	N
He can play baseball	Y	N
He is a Democrat	Y	N
He loves watermelon	Y	N
He grew up in a middle-class home	Y	N
He wears a durag	Y	N
He can't dance at all	Y	N
He wears large jewelry	Y	N
He loves comic books	Y	N
He loves rock 'n' roll	Y	N

Complete the tally. Rank the three boys. Who got the most yes votes? Who was "Blacker," Billy, Tyrone, or Michael? List them in order of who fits into Black culture the most. I had the class complete the activity as well. Who came out on top as the "Blackest" person, and who came out as the least "Blackest" person? Who do you think the class said would be considered the "Blackest," and who do you think the class said would be considered the least "Blackest?" The names of the three men also mattered, as the class pointed out. Billy is considered a name of White culture. Tyrone is considered a name of Black culture. The students also pointed out that my first name was a typical name for Black American culture. Michael, however, according to the class, could be a part of both Black OR White American culture. As my students unanimously pointed out, names are associated with culture.

A few of my Black students admitted that they have known Black Americans who were conflicted about what to name their babies. I asked what they were conflicted about? The students said that the parents wanted to name the child a traditional Black name (like Tyrone) but were afraid of how it would affect the child's future as it relates to finding employment if they put a Black sounding name on a resume. They said studies had shown that it is somewhat harder for Black Americans to get a high-paying job depending on their name as opposed to a White applicant with the exact same resume.

I have also heard of this dilemma from other Black Americans. To play devil's advocate, I brought up African immigrants. African immigrants from some West African countries are some of the most successful people in America. Look at a traditional Nigerian name. It sounds nothing like a typical American name, yet many Nigerian Americans have done tremendously well and have incredible jobs and careers. I mentioned that they had to put their names on a resume, yet it didn't hinder them from getting hired. However, one student brought up the aspect of subcultures as discussed earlier. The student said that because the name is completely different from a typical Black American name, a company may assume that the person is an immigrant. In many cases, immigrants are more respected than Black Americans because of the stereotype that immigrants are "hard workers" while Black Americans are lazy.

I mentioned the television show "The Fresh Prince of Bel-Air" earlier. One of the main characters is Carlton Banks. Carlton was the opposite of the main character, Will Smith. Will was from a tough neighborhood in West Philadelphia. His cousin Carlton grew up in Bel-Air, California, a wealthy neighborhood. Will was raised by a single mother. Carlton was raised "privileged" by two loving and well-off parents.

Will was into hip-hop. Carlton was into Barry Manilow. Will wore loud clothing, talked in "slang," could dance, played basketball, was tall and "cool." Carlton wore sweaters, used proper English, couldn't dance, wasn't athletic, was short, wasn't "cool," and was a Republican to top it off. Will's mother moved him from West Philadelphia to Bel-Air (hence the premise of the show) and the differences between the two was a major plotline of the show. Will would constantly ridicule Carlton for not being "Black" enough, while Carlton would constantly judge Will as being uncultured. The creators and the writers of the show clearly knew the angle they were playing. Watching the show, the audience was led to see Will as being "Black." They would look at Carlton, and basically the consensus was "he ain't Black." Will was looked at generally as being a part of Black culture, while Carlton, was not even identified as Black/African American.

I brought up the show to my class and everyone had seen and heard of the show. They liked the show also even though it was well before their era. There are quite a few episodes of the show that have always stood out to me. One such episode was from Season 4, Episode 8. The name of the episode is "Blood Is Thicker than Mud," but some refer to it as "Carlton Is a Sellout." In the episode, Will and Carlton are both trying to join a "Black" fraternity. One of the deans of the fraternity takes a liking to Will but is not too fond of Carlton because of the characteristics of Carlton that were described earlier. When the young men are pledging, the dean of the fraternity has Carlton do twice as much work as the other pledges, and the worst jobs as well. Will brings this up to Carlton, but Carlton ignores it and basically alludes to the fact that he wants to prove his worth. In fact, it is Carlton who seems to be most excited about joining this "Black" fraternity.

Weeks later, there is a party thrown by the frat for the pledges to congratulate them for making it into the fraternity. Will privately talks to the dean of the frat, who lets him know that he is in. Will assumes that he means Carlton also, but the dean of the frat tells him, not Carlton. Will is confused and asks why. The dean tells him "He ain't one of us," and he isn't the type suitable for that fraternity. Will becomes upset and tries to leave with Carlton, lying that HE did not get into the fraternity. Carlton goes to defend his cousin to the dean, which is when the dean reveals in front of everyone at the party that Will got in, but not Carlton. When Carlton asks why, the dean calls him a "sellout." Will attempts to fight the dean, but Carlton stops him. He asks the dean why he is a sellout. Again, the dean lists the adjectives of Carlton that the show played on.

Carlton tells him that being "Black isn't who I am trying to be; it is who I am." He explains to the dean that even though they may be different, they both have to jump through the same hoops and hurdles. He then tells the dean that HE is really the sellout for trying to tear down another Black person simply because he is different. He and Will leave and explain the situation to the rest of the family, who question why Black Americans still do this to each other.

The show's writers knew enough to expose the situation of how Black Americans can treat each other based on perceived judgments of who fits into "Black culture." Also, the fact that Will would relentlessly mock Carlton yet took more offense at the dean's insults of Carlton than Carlton did, showed that deep down, Will knew that his jokes all along were not right. I showed the clip to the class and asked them for their reaction. They felt that what they saw was wrong on the part of the dean and admitted it can be common among Black Americans. Have you seen this episode? What are your reactions to it? If you haven't, watch it if you can find it online.

Black Americans are not the only ones who are guilty of saying or alluding to Black Americans as not being Black or Black enough. Some non-Blacks are guilty of this also. As mentioned earlier, a recent presidential candidate who is White received a lot of criticism for telling Black voters that if they don't know whether to vote for him or his opponent then "they ain't Black." A few years earlier, another former presidential candidate who is also White, was giving an interview with a Black radio station. When asked by the interviewers, who were Black, what is one thing that she carries in her pocketbook, she responded with hot sauce. Many argued clearly both candidates were pandering to Black people. Some Black people believed she was playing on the stereotype that Black Americans love hot sauce. They were pandering to Black people not based on race, but on what is perceived to be Black culture. In their perception, true Black Americans culturally all vote one way, and love hot sauce, and if you vote the other way or you do not like hot sauce, then you can't be a part of Black culture. I showed this to the class. They were not too fond of it.

As mentioned earlier, one of my students explained that they heard that they weren't really Black because they lived in a nice neighborhood, which to most people means a "White" neighborhood. Part of Black culture stereotypically is growing up poor in the projects and overcoming extreme hurdles. This student never did that. I explained to the students that I've been reacted to in the same way. When I moved out of Brooklyn to Long Island to a nice house with a lawn, and my parents sent me to a private high school, some Black people would say I grew up White.

There were White people who would tell me that I did not grow up Black jokingly not realizing how insulting to Black people that is. In fact, many White people for some odd reason believe that I am rich, or that I grew up rich. It always baffled me why they would think that. I grew up in an average middle-class environment. My home was no smaller or bigger than a typical middle-class home on Long Island. However, to some White people, the fact that I could live in a nice neighborhood must mean that I am rich as a Black person, whereas a White person who grew up the exact same way was simply regular middle class.

Subconsciously, it was as if White people who assumed that I am rich believed that I should have grown up in "the hood." The fact that I grew up like them meant that I was well-off, even though they weren't. Subconsciously, maybe White money was better than Black money. Black culture is poor and struggling. White culture is middle class, private schools, and being safe. These White people didn't realize how insulting they were being. And they weren't joking when they assumed I was rich.

The student could relate, and he said it greatly annoyed him when people made the same assumptions about him. A White person who grows up middle class goes to a private school, and isn't in poverty is a part of White culture. A Black person who grows up the same way isn't part of "Black" culture. Little did they know that when my parents moved to this country, we lived in a rough environment in Brooklyn, and they worked their way up to get our family to Long Island, and provide a great life for my sister and I. My early upbringing WAS the stereotypical Black upbringing, but they were only seeing the results of hardwork on the part of my parents. The class did not like this and took it as insulting as well. Should Black Americans be insulted by these generalizations of Black culture from both White AND Black people?

CULTURAL APPROPRIATION

As an activity, I told the class that we would go around the room, and I would point to a person, and they would tell me if they considered that person a part of Black culture. I started with myself, and the students said yes, obviously. I asked them how on earth it was obvious. They started to say that I was Black, but before they could I pointed out that some of them had admitted that they had told other Black people that they were not a part of Black culture. One student said that I liked hip-hop music because I had talked about hip-hop in class before. I pointed out, however, that I may like a song in hip-hop, but it doesn't necessarily mean I like hip-hop. One student said that I like fried chicken from a previous discussion, but again if a White man likes fried chicken also does that make them a part of Black culture? The students did not know much about my personal life outside of what I may have told them so how could they possibly know enough about me to determine my true culture?

I went around the room and pointed at each student and asked the rest of the class if they believed that student was a part of Black culture. When we got to the Native American student the class said yes, however, the Native American student disagreed and said she did not consider herself part of Black culture. I asked the class if they can truly determine a person's "culture" just by looking at them.

So, culture does not necessarily have to do with race. They can be two totally different things. One student who frequently visited the class even though she wasn't enrolled in the course brought up a popular term in Black culture. She brought up the words "Cultural Appropriation." I wanted to ask the class if non-Blacks can be members of

Black culture. Before posing the question I asked them if they knew what cultural appropriation was. Do you know what it is? As always, let's define:

> *-cultural appropriation takes place when members of a majority group adopt cultural elements of a minority group in an exploitative, disrespectful, or stereotypical way (Britannica)*
>
> *-the adoption, usually without acknowledgment, of cultural identity markers from subcultures or minority communities into mainstream culture by people with a relatively privileged status (Dictionary.com)*
>
> *-a term used to describe the taking over of creative or artistic forms, themes, or practices by one cultural group from another (Oxford)*
>
> *-when people from a dominant culture adopt the practices, language, artistic expression, etc., of a non-dominant culture without fully understanding or appreciating them (Macmillan Dictionary)*

After analyzing the definitions, the class came to a consensus that cultural appropriation is when members of a particular culture use another culture to their advantage for the purpose of making money, even though they really do not relate to that culture. For example, White Americans wearing cornrows, a popular hairstyle in Black American culture. Another example is White Americans making music that is associated with Black culture. We even looked at some images of this. One student brought up Elvis Presley and rock and roll as an example of cultural appropriation, saying that rock and roll was originally Black music. The students were not big fans of cultural appropriation. They believed it to be inauthentic when a person from one culture takes on another culture and benefits from it more than the particular people of the culture they were copying.

I wanted to point something out, however. How are we determining who is a part of what culture? For example, the White American wearing cornrows. Who says that he or she was not raised in Black culture? Who says that he or she didn't grow up among Black Americans? Or learned about Black culture to the point they were "Blacker" than some Black people that the same students would point out "ain't really Black?"

One assignment that was given to the class was on residents of East Jackson, Ohio. They were "White"; however, they said that they were Black due to their "culture." They were raised Black, so they identified as Black. What if a White or Asian orphan is adopted by Black parents? Are they a part of Black culture? What if a Black orphan is adopted by Asian parents? Are they part of Black culture? Although members of the class felt that race was highly important when analyzing culture, it was not everything. Culture is how you are raised deep down and what identity you go with.

Questions To Consider/Answer

How would you describe Black American culture? What are its "characteristics?"

How do you feel about Black culture in general?

Can non-Blacks be members of Black American culture? How so?

What are your thoughts on cultural appropriation?

Who determines what culture a person belongs to: the members of that culture OR *the specific individual?*

CHAPTER TEN

BLACK AMERICANS: VICTIMS OR VICTORS?

Perspective is extremely important. Two people can see the exact same thing and interpret it completely differently. Our experiences, our ages, how we were raised, our finances, where we grew up, our parents, our friends, our gender, how our brains work and so many other things can play a role in how we see things. Perspective is a part of critical thinking. You need to have a perspective AND acknowledge that there are always other perspectives. Truly, our perspective on things will guide our decision-making, our emotions, and our behavior. I've mentioned perspective quite a few times, but I haven't defined it. We will do that now. What is the definition of perspective? Let's go to the dictionary.

-a mental view or prospect

-the interrelation in which a subject or its parts are mentally viewed

-the capacity to view things in their true relations or relative importance (Merriam-Webster)

-the state of one's ideas, the facts known to one etc…in having a meaningful interrelationship (Dictionary.com)

-a particular way of viewing things that depends on one's experience and personality (Cambridge English Dictionary)

-a way of thinking about and understanding something (Britannica)

-your perspective is the way you see something (Vocabulary.com)

-a way of thinking about something; sensible way of judging a situation (Macmillan)

-a way of regarding situations, facts, etc. and judging their relative importance (The Free Dictionary)

The definitions were very similar, however, the two definitions of perspective the class really wanted to adhere to were the definitions from Cambridge and Vocabulary.com. As our minds have been shaped that we are all different races and cultures in America (indoctrination maybe?), it is impossible for Americans not to have different perspectives on the same things. Of course, experiences play a huge role in this. Black Americans may have a different perspective on issues than White or Asian Americans. However, what may be even more important is the perspectives of Black Americans themselves.

As I am writing this portion of the book, the 2021-2022 school year is ending. The class discussed and debated many different topics that of course are not mentioned in this book. One of the last topics for discussion forms this chapter. From the dawn of the United States to the present day and even into the future, are Black Americans Victims of America or Victors in America? How should Black Americans view themselves? More importantly, how do my students view themselves? ESPECIALLY my Black/African American students? What was their perspective? What is your perspective?

Now the easy cop-out answer is that Black Americans are both victims and victors. And yes, Black Americans are victims and victors. One could argue both. However, it is hard to believe that people in their minds put Black Americans as equally both. Everyone has a bias, and in perspective, bias most certainly plays a part. After everything discussed in the course, and after all the analyzing and different perspectives, I wanted to get my students' perspectives on how they view Black Americans, and how America should view Black Americans as well. How one views oneself can be key to their future. Of course, there are pros and cons to both perspectives. We analyzed both perspectives, and each student had to pick one.

Black Americans, Victims or Victors?

VICTIMS

As always, before discussing a topic we must first look up the definition in the dictionary. So, what is a victim? As a class, we looked it up:

-one that is acted on and usually adversely affected by a force or agent (Merriam-Webster)

-someone or something that has been hurt, damaged, or killed or has suffered either because of the actions of someone or something else, or because of illness or chance (Cambridge)

-a person who suffers from a destructive or injurious action or agency (Dictionary.com)

-someone who has suffered as a result of someone else's actions or beliefs, or as a result of unpleasant circumstances (Collins English Dictionary)

-someone who has been harmed by crime; person who has suffered from someone's actions (Macmillan Dictionary)

-a person who has been attacked, injured, robbed, or killed by someone else; a person who is cheated or fooled by someone else (Britannica)

Many Black Americans as well as other Americans view Black/African Americans as victims in America. Given a basic understanding of American history, you could see why. I asked the class to explain why Black Americans would or could be considered victims in America. They pointed out the obvious reasons. Years of slavery, slave codes, lynchings, unjust trials and imprisonment, Jim Crow laws, segregation, and police brutality. They had a long list of evidence that Black Americans were victims. Black Americans have been the victims of denial of opportunity for most of American history. We discussed land that has been taken away from Black Americans that provided or could have provided wealth for them and their families. Also, Black communities in the past that were destroyed by outside forces.

Black Americans have lower levels of wealth than White Americans partially because they were denied equal opportunities to build wealth due to redlining and mortgage denials over the years. It was pointed out that Black Americans make up a disproportionate number of inmates in America's prison system. According to prisonpolicy.org as of 2018, African Americans make up 13% of the United States population; however, they make up 38% of the people in prison. The incarceration rate for Black Americans is 2,306 per 100,000 people versus 450 per 100,000 people for White Americans. The arrest rate for Black vs. White Americans was 6,109 vs. 2,795 per 100,000. The percentage of people on probation or on parole who are Black is around 30%.

I asked the class if Black Americans were that disproportionately violent compared to other Americans and they said they did not believe so. I asked if it were possible that some Black Americans were victims of a justice system that might not have been fair to some Blacks simply because they were Black, and they said absolutely. Some students pointed out that things still exist to this day that happened 50, 75, and over 100 years ago to Black Americans. We looked at a recent article from Bloomberg.com about Wells Fargo Bank, which was caught denying more than qualified Black applicants for loans that were given to equally qualified White applicants. We also discussed the War on Drugs of the 1970s and the Violent Crime Control and Law Enforcement Acts of the 1990s that led to skyrocketing incarceration rates for Blacks. Black men especially and disproportionately, as pointed out, were the victims of these laws. The constant fight for civil rights was also pointed out. Some students even mentioned that Black Americans have been the victims of cultural appropriation. All these things were brought up and are true.

I asked the students if Black Americans were also victimized by other Black Americans. I mentioned the fact of gang violence in Black communities (which was discussed in the class) and how many of the deaths of Black Americans are caused by other Black Americans. In certain inner-city neighborhoods Black people today can most certainly be considered victims. The attacks on Black Americans not only come from outside forces but many of them today come from within. The class agreed. Gentrification is another case that students brought up about Black Americans today becoming victims. African Americans in many neighborhoods believe they are being priced out of these areas and displaced on purpose. Again, a person could do their own research and get an endless list of how Black Americans have been treated historically in America and conclude that Black Americans are most certainly victims in this country.

If an African American looks at themselves as a victim, it may make them more aware of their current situation. They may be on the lookout for "abuse" or be more cautious in their dealings. For example, if a person has been victimized by the police, they may know what pattern to look for when dealing with an officer who may be abusive and act accordingly. That is one argument. Also, one could argue that if you are the victim of something, it may make or force you to get treatment or help. If a person is a victim of being thrown into a swimming pool and they cannot swim and they almost drown, they may then afterward learn how to swim so they are never victims of drowning again.

Mental health among Black Americans is now being discussed more frequently. According to statistics from goodtherapy.org, Black Americans are the least likely racial or cultural group to go for therapy. This is especially true of Black men. Black male suicide rates have been reported as rising faster than that of any other racial or gender group in the United States currently. Why is this? The class discussed it. A few students said that therapy is not discussed much in Black American culture, but they didn't really have an answer for why. Very rarely do victims not need help to overcome their trauma. If a person has been victimized, then they may need help. If Black Americans view themselves as victims, then more Black Americans should be seeking help, was the class consensus. Maybe if Black Americans viewed themselves as victims, they would then get the help they need to overcome the trauma they are dealing with. This is one perspective.

Another perspective is if Black Americans constantly view themselves as victims, it may hinder their progress. Many people in life love to blame others for their problems, or "play the victim" card. One famous instance of this is the "blame the White man" syndrome. Many Blacks have argued that too many other Blacks suffer from this to justify their lack of success. Some Blacks believe they are the "victims" of White Americans. Are Black Americans today actually victims? We know that Black Americans in previous centuries were victims (not necessarily individually). However, are Black Americans victims TODAY? One student mentioned that slavery had a traumatic effect on Black Americans that is still being felt to this day. A few other students agreed. I asked the student to explain how slavery from over 150 years ago impacted them. Some students said the trauma of slavery was passed down from generation to generation.

I asked my students if they were victims of slavery, how could they explain the nice shoes they were wearing, the nice cell phones they were using, or all the social media platforms they were a part of? I asked them if they were the victims of slavery, or if actual slaves were the victims of slavery. I also asked them if it was disrespectful for African Americans today to use slavery as an excuse for victimhood. They asked me to explain. I pointed out that slaves had a very rough life. If a slave from the past saw how my students were living (advanced technology, free education, a BLACK teacher for example), would they appreciate them saying that Black Americans today have it rough, and they are victims today because of what former slaves went through?

How can Black Americans complain about the trauma of slavery when not a single Black American was alive during the era of slavery in the United States?

If my great-grandfather had been abused, does his trauma affect me in any way? Well, as a student pointed out, it may be if my great-grandfather's abuse is passed down to my grandfather who then abuses my father who abuses me, sure. However, if my grandfather stops the abuse, then can I really relate to the trauma of abuse that my great-grandfather went through? Could I not argue the same for slavery? If I asked the average Black student to write a five-page paper without research on slavery in America, many would not be able to do it as they are too far detached from that time. If that is the case, do they then really know the trauma of slavery if they can barely describe it?

African Americans are known to spend exorbitant amounts of money on material wealth. I showed the class a Forbes article titled "The 300 Billion Black American Consumerism Bag Breeds Big Business Opportunities" written by Kori Hale in September 2021 about the spending power of Black Americans. According to the numbers detailed in the article, Black Americans make up approximately 48 million people in the United States. African Americans are the second largest consumer group in America and account for about 10% of household spending as of the year 2019. In 2019, Black consumer expenditures in America totaled around $835 billion, which is more money than Spain, Turkey, Mexico, and Switzerland generate annually. African Americans statistically are also known to purchase luxury items and beauty products at a disproportionate rate to their household income. Most Americans spend outside of their means, but is it possible that Black Americans do it at the most disproportionate rate? I asked the class if African Americans can be considered victims while driving luxury cars, having fake hair, or nice handbags. Is a person with the latest Air Jordans or newest cell phone, or a designer belt that is simply used for holding up one's jeans, really a victim? Have Black Americans been victimized? In the history of America, absolutely. Are Black Americans today really victims?

Many people, as I explained to the class, who are non-Black and who are Black as well say that too many Black Americans have a "victim" mentality that holds them back. They focus on past injustices that hold them back from future progress. I once heard an anecdote that I shared with the class to give them a different look at things. Imagine you were in a car accident where you were hit by a drunk driver. You survive, but lose the ability to walk. The drunk driver is sued and convicted, and you win money; however, for you to walk again, you must go to years of physical therapy. Nobody can walk for you. You must learn to walk yourself, even though you did nothing to put yourself in this situation. It was due to the negligence of the drunk driver. As much as the court can punish the drunk driver in your favor, what they cannot do is have the drunk driver who caused your condition walk for you. You must learn how to walk again regardless of whether it was your fault or not. You can blame the drunk driver all day, but in the end, it is up to you to get up, go to physical therapy, and walk again in the future as you once did in the past.

Is blaming the drunk driver forever and being the victim going to help you, or is getting up on your own two feet and relearning how to walk again going to help you? Is blaming the "White man" or the American government and constantly playing the victim going to help you as a Black American OR is taking ownership of your life after some of the progress that has been made over the course of American history in favor of Black Americans better for your future?

Black/African Americans who believe they are victims have been hurt, but who is responsible to get Black Americans to walk again? Is it the White man? Is it the government? Or is it on us? I asked the class if African Americans were the only victims in America, and they said of course not. Was slavery only something that existed in America? Again, they responded no. Africa has had slavery since before America's beginnings and well after America abolished it, yet Africans do not focus on slavery at the same rate as African Americans. Why is this? Will constantly thinking of yourself as a victim help you? It could make you more aware and prepared for future injustices, or it can hinder you and halt your future. I asked the class what they thought. It was challenging for the class to answer. Most of the students believed the victim identity to be bad; however, a couple of students believed that a victim should always acknowledge when they are victims of cruelty so as not to allow it to happen again. What do you think?

VICTORS

Next, we looked up the word victor in various dictionaries. A victor is defined as:

-one that defeats an enemy or opponent; a winner (Merriam-Webster)

-a person who has overcome an adversary, conqueror; a winner in any struggle or contest (Dictionary.com)

-the winner in a battle or struggle (Collins Dictionary)

-a person who defeats an enemy or opponent (Britannica)

We also looked up the word victorious. Similarly, to victor, victorious is defined as:

-having won a victory; winning; triumphant (Collins dictionary)

What would happen if Black Americans looked at themselves as victors, instead of victims? I posed this question to the class. Going back to the days of slavery until now, have Black Americans been victorious in many ways? No doubt Black Americans have historically had several enemies in this country. One cannot deny that. Have African Americans not had several victories along the way? I discussed the slave rebellions that occurred during the days of slavery. Even though many failed and the battles may have been lost, in the end, chattel slavery was abolished.

Again, we did discuss whether slavery ever really did end. Today however, none of my students nor I myself were slaves, so that was a victory. I discussed the many inventions produced by Black Americans during times when everything was done to hinder Black progress. Were these not victories? We talked about the civil rights movement, and the Voting Rights Acts of the 1960s. We discussed both the 14th and 15th Amendments. We discussed the history of Black churches and businesses and communities being burned down and terrorized, yet Black businesses exist here in America and Black churches do as well. I asked the class if they got on a bus or a plane, would they be forced to sit in the back? Absolutely not, they responded. Is that not a victory for Black Americans as well? As discussed earlier, my class is a mix of Native American, Hispanic, AND Black students. Didn't many Black Americans in the past want to end legal segregation? There are African American members of Congress who create laws. In 2008 the United States elected a Black president. Most African Americans believed they would never see the day that would happen here in the United States. Many Black Americans work in high-paying professions and do amazing things that are often not highlighted. The list of the tremendous successes of Black Americans in this nation goes on and on. From one perspective, with all the struggles that African Americans have had to deal with, some would say that Black Americans are victors.

As always, however, I wanted to highlight another perspective. If Black Americans today are victors, does that make them victorious? And if they are victorious, does that mean there are no more battles or struggles to endure? According to TheBlackWallStTimes.com in 2017, since the 1960s, fewer Black children are living in two-parent households than before the 1960s. Also since the 1960s, Black marriages have declined and are continuing to decline at disproportionate rates. Are these signs of progress? Would these be considered victories? The percentage of African Americans in prison has recently started to decline, but many would argue it is still disproportionately high. Also, crime in many Black neighborhoods is high today. These are all according to blackdemographics.com, which the class analyzed together. Are Black people truly victorious?

If Black people view themselves as victors, is it possible it could hinder their progress moving forward? Is it possible Black Americans who view themselves as victors stop trying to advance and become satisfied, even lazy, in how they operate moving forward? I discussed with the class that Black Americans today, one could argue, are the most comfortable they have ever been in American society. Could that be why Black Americans today are stereotyped as lazy? Could it be that they believe they are victorious, and the struggle has ended? How would past civil rights leaders look at African Americans today? Would they be happy with what they saw?

Nobody will ever know. I asked the class how would great Black Americans, from Frederick Douglass, Booker T. Washington, Carter

G. Woodson, Ella Baker, Ida Wells, W.E.B. Du Bois, Marcus Garvey, Medgar Evers, Malcolm X, Martin Luther King Jr., Fred Hampton, and many other Black heroes view Black Americans now? Many of these individuals had differing beliefs, but wanted to see Black Americans progress and were part of the struggle to make that happen. If they saw Black Americans today, would they view them as victors, as a consensus? What do you think?

I asked my Black students how they viewed Black people. I asked them, most importantly, how they view themselves. They could only choose one. Are you a victim or a victor? Out of eight students, five students believed that they were victors. Three believed that they were victims here in America. When examining Black Americans as a whole, they were split evenly between victims and victors. I asked the students who believed Black Americans were victims, who were the victimizers. They responded everyone, including other Black Americans. It wasn't the stereotypical response of the "White man" that they claimed many Blacks like to use in their arguments of why Blacks are victims.

Questions To Consider/Answer

How do you view Black/African Americans, as Victims or Victors (Choose one)? Explain why.

If you are a Black/African American, how do you view yourself? As a Victim or a Victor (Choose one) Explain why.

AFTERWORD

As I write, the first year of the Black Experience in America is ending. The topics discussed in this book are only a fraction of all the things that we discussed in class. The final assignment of the course asked the students to explain to me what they got out of the course and how it may have impacted them. I believe most high school courses do not have a major impact on the lives of students. I'm hoping that this course will. I wanted to do something different, which is why I created this course. The students and I both found the course to be a tremendous success. With minimal promotion, the class is expected to have more students on the roster for the second year of the class's existence. In fact, the roster is projected to more than double for next school year. I have Black, Hispanic, AND White students signed up for next year. That really excites me. I am glad people have realized that this is not a course just for Black people. It is a course for all, and ALL perspectives are needed. I had students who were not in the course give up their free periods to willingly come in and check out the class. How often do students give up their free time to go to a class they are not enrolled in to learn something new instead of hanging out with friends? What do you think?

The negative feedback that I had expected never came. At least not publicly. Members of the community were almost universally supportive. In early October 2021, my principal contacted me to let me know that the district's local paper wanted to do an article about the course. This was the moment I had been waiting for. Almost 99% of the community had no idea what I was doing. In fact, 99% of the teachers in my building had no idea what I was doing. The reporter had heard of the class from a Zoom meeting on DEI (Diversity, Equity, and Inclusivity) that I was a part of, in which my assistant superintendent informed the few members of the meeting about the new course. One of the members of the meeting wrote for the local paper and showed interest and contacted my high school principal. This article would bring the class out publicly. Reluctantly, I agreed. I had prepared myself for this moment. I was ready for the backlash. For 19 years, 99% of the people in the community had no idea who I was. This would change that.

I conducted the interview by phone from my principal's office. He was in the meeting with me for support. My district completely supported me along the way in this process, and this was no different. The interview lasted about 40 minutes. I thought it went well. I described the course, my vision, why I created the course, how it operated, etc. A few weeks later, the article was posted. I read the article. I refused to read the comments online. Quite a few people from the community, and some other teachers, were surprised. They had been unaware of the new course. They told me that almost all the comments were positive, from the ENTIRE community. In fact, one teacher told me it was the first time ever she saw everyone in the comment section agree on something, without any nasty vitriol. I was shocked.

Some teachers were supportive. Some said nothing. Over my career, some teachers and former administrators never really looked at me as a good teacher. Why? My assumption is that my methods were a little different. I like to think outside the box. I love to bring a different perspective. Certain teachers are great at lesson planning and sticking to it, leaving no wiggle room for anything outside of the plan. I was different. I loved when my lesson went in a different direction with my students because it meant they were thinking critically. Critical thinking doesn't fit into a lesson plan. The lesson goes where the discussion leads. For the most part, my students loved my classes. That's all I cared about. In fact, the same teachers who didn't think highly of me as a teacher were the same teachers many of my students complained about.

I always had an open-door policy for this class. Any adult could come in to observe and take part at any time. The reason for this was full transparency. I wanted members of the community to know that I was not indoctrinating the students at all. The students would never know my position, or belief, on a particular subject. No matter what they said, I was going to question them and challenge them. Even if I agreed with the student, I would debate them and find flaws in their belief as if I disagreed. When the students asked me what I thought about a particular issue or subject, I wouldn't tell them. I wanted to teach them to THINK FOR THEMSELVES. I didn't want to indoctrinate them. "The Black Experience in America" is a tool for me to do so. As the months went on in the school year, some teachers, security guards, and even community members came into the class. Every superintendent came in as well. Other teachers expressed interest in coming in when they had the chance. Each one told me they had never seen a class like this before. Many of them would even share an article or a video they thought would be useful for the course.

A teacher I was close with would bring up my class in his class. He said many of the students were interested in the subject matter. I would stop into his class and talk about some of the things we discussed in my class. Not for long, but just drop little seeds. As scheduling started for the following school year (2022-2023) I had a few students who came up to me and showed interest in taking the course. When the course was "African American History and Literature," students were mostly placed into the class. Now, students were asking to join. Again, I wanted to keep the numbers low. I had different types of students ask to join. I had some AP students. I had Black, Hispanic, AND White students who were eager to join. Even though the course is called "The Black Experience in America," it was open to everyone. The course is just a tool to look at issues through the eyes of Black Americans. I had one student during the school year who would try to cut her other class that period to sit in on the course. She would sit in and participate as if she were getting credit for the course, even though she wasn't. I had students interested in taking the course the following year give up their free period to sit in on the course. The feedback was positive. Even students who couldn't take the class because of their schedule loved the concept and said that we needed more classes like this.

The class was gaining some popularity. In less than one year, the class was already more popular than years of the "African American History and Literature" course. I had nine students originally scheduled to take the course the next school year (2022-2023) and that is where I wanted to cap it. Again, I wanted intimacy. By the start of the new school year, 18 were signed up to take the course. I felt this was too much, but I am willing to give it a try. Not everyone is ready for this course. Some other students showed interest but could not take it because their grades were too low in their core subjects (remember this course is an elective). The community so far has shown support. My deepest fears never came to fruition. I was wrong about my previous assumptions. I gained more and more confidence. Being this was the course's first year, there are things that will change moving forward. I've had one guest speaker this year. The guest speaker was a parent of one of the students in the class (another Black male teacher in our district) who spoke on his experience as a Black Man working in our district. In the future, I plan to have more.

As the 2021-2022 school year drew to a close, I was extremely happy with the first year of the course. There were several topics that we were unable to touch upon as we had run out of time. I explained to the class that the statistics that were brought up in class should not be the end all be all of a discussion as statistics can always be manipulated. However, they can be helpful in being used as a guideline for debate and discussion. Moving forward, I hope to analyze more statistics if I have more time. Maybe in the future, the course will go from a half-year course to a full-year course. I don't want to get ahead of myself. The fact the course exists as it does, I will most certainly accept for now. The students are the driving force behind the class, not me. We went with the flow. If they wanted to discuss something, we discussed it. There were no "boxes" to fit into.

Again, critical thinking does not fit into a box. It is outside the box, which is what I encourage. It's the premise of the class. I was just a facilitator of discussion. My students truly inspired me. I am proud of them beyond words. They always had my back even when I had doubts about what I was doing in running the course. The class has given me a new purpose in education, which after 19 to 20 years in a career, a person needs at times. After this school year, I will have 13 years left in education before retirement. I sincerely hope the course continues those 13 years. Will it? Who knows where we will be one year from now, let alone 13. If I only get to teach this course for one or two years, it will have been worth it.

Students would always try to guess what my beliefs were based on discussions. I always reminded them they have no idea what I think. Of course, with every topic discussed in the class, and this book, I have my own perspective. Remember, you do not know it. And you never will. Just because I say something does not mean I agree with it. It is just to facilitate discussion and critical thinking. My students do not know my perspectives on 99% of the topics discussed in the class. I did make a couple of exceptions when discussing my personal experiences as a Black/African American. I was able to keep my perspectives out of the class so as not to indoctrinate my students. I want them to think for themselves

In 19 years of teaching, I finally feel that I am doing something different. The course gave me new inspiration in the middle of a long teaching career. As much as I tried to avoid it, the more it found me. The faster I ran from it, the faster it caught up to me. It was meant to happen, so it happened no matter what I did. I was happy I was wrong. "The Black Experience in America for Secondary Education" was official. I could do what I've always wanted to do. Teach. I sincerely thank the school district where I work for allowing me the opportunity to teach this course, as most schools do not have the guts for anything like this in my opinion. Also, I thank them for believing in me as being competent enough to make this work, as our high school had never had anything like this before.

I must admit, though, that I am extremely worried about the United States. I won't get into specifics, but there are things that greatly concern me. Our nation is extremely divided and many in this country refuse to look at things from different perspectives. This can help to create a divide among people. If this nation does not address its issues, we will have serious problems. If people in this country cannot understand that there are different perspectives on things and simply respect that, how can we move forward as a nation? I mentioned the Pledge of Allegiance earlier. Recite the Pledge of Allegiance and analyze it. Are we as a nation practicing the words that are being recited? What do you think?

If there is any hope, perhaps that lies with my students. They were wonderful, and words cannot express how proud I am of them. I truly hope as they have now graduated from our high school, they take what they have learned and discussed, and it helps them grow into wonderful adults. The last couple of days of the course, most of the students told me that the course had a tremendous impact on them. The students said that what they really enjoyed about the course was the ability to speak freely, to be challenged, and to have an open forum where they were not judged for their thoughts. They all remarked that they loved the concept of critical thinking, and no course they had taken in high school had stressed that regularly. They also loved that the class only had eight students (nine unofficially, counting the student who came whenever she could get out of her other class) and they loved the intimacy of the discussion. I received some gifts and cards from some of the students in the class. One of the cards read:

"Three years ago, when I first sat in your class, I never understood how important and how influential your teaching would inspire me. Because of you, I strongly believe that teachers like you are extremely rare. Not only me, but every last student that has entered and left your classes feels the same exact way. Prepared. You have allowed me to look at things from a different perspective and allowed me to express myself freely without any judgment. This is exactly why you are the most perfect fit for The Black Experience! Everything that comes your way is very well deserved and I hope to give you your flowers while you can still smell them. So, thank you so much for everything! You're an inspiration to many people, including myself!"

One of the many wonderful compliments I received, and truly inspirational to hear such kind words from a student. I hope my students continue to think outside the box and stave off indoctrination, and embrace critical thinking. As I always tell my students; If you always think like the average person, then you can always expect to be the average person.

I hope my course and this book help create change. Will it do so? Honestly, I do not believe so. The indoctrination of Americans is too deep. However, I do hope this course can inspire individuals to do better for themselves and to think for themselves as well. I only decided to do this course if I could help create a change. Helping others is great but changing them for the better is fantastic. If I gave a homeless, unemployed man $10, did I help him? Sure, I did. In the end, he is still homeless and jobless. If I teach him a skill and help him get a job, that's change. That is what I hope this course can accomplish. I don't want to just help students; I want to change them for the better. I can't change our nation, but I can help change individuals. If I can manage to do that, then "The Black Experience in America For Secondary Education" will have done its job. Think back to your days in high school or look at your child's school. Do they have many courses or opportunities like this? If they don't, why not? Could it be beneficial? What do you think?

ACKNOWLEDGEMENTS AND THANK YOU'S

Natacha Boyce- Thank you for pushing me even when I didn't want to be pushed and for being my strongest advocate.

Mark and Marlene Boyce- Thank you for never giving up on me, even when I gave you every reason to. Thank you for giving me more than I deserve.

Shauna Boyce- Thank you for being the best sister in the world.

Thanks to those who believed in me even when I didn't believe in myself:

Jennifer Palermo

Steven Chudyk

Eddie Moujaber

Thanks to those behind the scenes who had my back:

Iquell Reina

Jimmy Richardson

Cynthia Richardson

Willie Austin

Peter Brown

Marilyn Banks Winter

James Banks

Greg Wallace

Robert Brandi

Riverhead Chapter of the NAACP

Riverhead Chapter of the AAECF

Thank You to the Riverhead Central School District, The Board of Education, and the High School Administration for taking a risk and allowing me this opportunity. Hoping more school districts follow your example.

Thank You to my family members, friends, students and inner circle who showed me tremendous support, and encouraged me to take this risk.

Thank you to the colleagues who showed support for the class. You know who you are.

Special thanks to:

Azharia Allen

Alicia Garner

Jaden Hopkins

Ariana Jackson

Jaylen Lee

Carter Richardson

Rachel Rojas

Ashna Snowden

Jazz Bey

You will never be forgotten. I hope life treats you as wonderful as you have treated me. Thank you.

www.ingramcontent.com/pod-product-compliance
Lightning Source LLC
Chambersburg PA
CBHW070625030426
42337CB00020B/3923